SUNSHINE

Our Gift of Love
SUNSHINE

by
B. R. Schmalzried, Sr.

With Foreword by
C. Everett Koop, M.D., ScD.

ST. PAUL EDITIONS

For *Part One*, originally published as *Sunshine—A Slow Miracle*, © 1965 by the Daughters of St. Paul:

NIHIL OBSTAT:
   Rev. Berthold Sehuk
IMPRIMATUR:
   ✠ Emmet M. Walsh
   Bishop of Youngstown

For *Part Two:*

NIHIL OBSTAT:
   Rev. Richard V. Lawlor, S.J.
IMPRIMATUR:
   ✠ Humberto Cardinal Medeiros
   Archbishop of Boston

Library of Congress Cataloging in Publication Data
Schmalzried, B. R.
   Sunshine, Our Gift of Love.

   1. Schmalzried, Mary Margaret, 1956-
2. Down's syndrome—Biography. I. Title.
HQ773.7.S26   1982   306.8'7[B]   82-22036
                                              AACR2

ISBN 0-8198-6830-2 (cloth)
      0-8198-6831-0 (paper)

Printed in the U.S.A. by the Daughters of St. Paul
50 St. Paul's Ave., Boston, MA 02130

The Daughters of St. Paul are an international congregation of religious women serving the Church with the communications media.

Acknowledgments

I am grateful to many individuals who encouraged me to write the story of my daughter, Mary Margaret, who has truly been "Sunshine" not only to my family but to countless others.

My special appreciation is extended to:

—Rev. A. Patrick Depmster, my parish priest, for encouraging me to write the accounts of Mary Margaret, and also for giving me some valuable tips on constructive writing.

—Sister Mary Rose Kohn, D.C., and Sister Lucille Marie Beauchamp, D.C., for their precious time spent in editing and typing the manuscript.

—Frances Ryan, a dear friend and neighbor, for retyping the original manuscript, *Sunshine—A Slow Miracle*.

—Tom Sheehan, a Youngstown State student, for the many photographs which he took that appear in this book.

B. R. Schmalzried, Sr.

Slow Miracle

How often do we look upon God as our last and feeblest hope! We turn to Him at the eleventh hour because we have no other recourse. And then we learn from Him that the storms of life have driven us, not upon the jagged rocks, but into a haven of bliss.

B. R. Schmalzried, Sr.

Contents

PART ONE
A Slow Miracle

PART TWO

Messenger of God's Love

Foreword

The man who stops his car for the red traffic light condemns the driver in the next car who slides through the signal. This story of the interaction between a mongoloid child and her family stands as an example of an achievable goal for parents of such youngsters and is all the more telling because the child in question is of low ability as it can be measured against the performance of other mongoloid children.

This is an appropriate time in history for this book to appear. Depicting the love and concern of a family for their mongoloid daughter, it stands as a monument to our old Judeo-Christian ethic of the sanctity of human life which is rapidly being supplanted in our secular humanistic society by a quality-of-life ethic.

I say the time is appropriate because unborn mongoloid babies are now the victims of the search-and-destroy mission of amniocentesis. Those who are born, if they have a life-threatening anomaly in addition to their mongolism, are more often than not provided with no surgical treatment so that they die. It is against this background that this simple story becomes so poignant.

One worth of the worthless is that they prove whether or not we are worthy to care for them. The broken hearts of parents for their defective child are frequently used to strengthen other hearts and to be an example of courage to those less courageous. Extraordinary gifts reward those who live with and for the handicapped. A greater dimension of love is found under these circumstances, for example, than is possible in any other way.

In spite of the fact that we live in a fallen world, a retarded infant is still a person created in the image of God. I have spent the major portion of my professional life concerned with infants born with congenital defects, treating them surgically and rehabilitating them into society as children. Some of these youngsters are mentally retarded as well as physically imperfect. As I face their care as a surgeon, I take comfort in the words that God spoke to Moses at the burning bush: "Who gave man his mouth? Who makes him deaf or dumb? Who gives him sight or makes him blind? Is it not I, the Lord?"

C. Everett Koop, M.D., ScD.

U.S. Surgeon General
and Deputy Assistant Secretary for Health

Co-author of the book and film series,
Whatever Happened to the Human Race?

Purpose

God in His love and wisdom knows our capabilities and would never permit us to shoulder a cross we cannot carry. True, sometimes the cross is mighty heavy, and we may stumble under its weight; but God in His mercy is forever waiting to offer a helping hand if we only have the faith to reach out for His divine assistance.

So it is that because God loves every one of us so much, be we millionaire or steelworker, debutante or salesgirl, He presents each of us the trial which will temper us for eternity.

Some of these misfortunes do not appear to make any sense at all; they seem to have no rational or moral content. Therefore, to millions of persons, because they lack faith in God, these experiences, particularly the more tragic ones, are most difficult to understand and to accept. They refuse to believe or accept anything that is beyond their finite powers of reasoning. Their attitude toward life is one of cynicism in which material things only are of importance. They are unaware of the misguided thinking that governs their lives.

But there are others who do have faith and therefore pray to God for strength and surcease. Some prayers are answered in the way requested. Others are answered in a manner we do not comprehend. And sometimes the blessings received are greater than those petitioned.

Through this little true story, *Sunshine— Our Gift of Love,* we hope the reader will find increased faith in and love of God, continued strength for daily Christian living, encouragement to shoulder the cross, and the comfort that comes when the bright sun of God's wisdom burns through our clouded thinking and leaves us to bask in the warmth of His love.

To Our Readers

Sixteen years have passed since the original story, *Sunshine—A Slow Miracle,* was published. During all these years many interesting events have taken place both spiritually and physically, not only to the Schmalzried family, but to many others. We are anxious and happy for everyone to share in these beautiful experiences as we are sure that you will enjoy them immensely. But for your reading pleasure and convenience, we, therefore, decided it best to print them as an addendum (Part Two) to the original story (Part One) in this handy volume.

PART ONE

A Slow Miracle

A Slow Miracle

It is good that heaven reveals to man the book of life just one page at a time. For if I had known what was written in the book for me, I would have climbed the walls, instead of just nervously pacing the floors, in the smoke-filled maternity waiting room at Youngstown North Side Hospital, that 29th day of May, 1956.

The event which was to have such a profound effect on my life was triggered when Doctor Allan Altdoerffer stepped into the room at 10:53 A.M. A welcome sight indeed—the waiting was over! As he approached, I noticed his usual radiant smile was missing, which gave me the impression that something was wrong. As he pulled a chair closer to me, he spoke in a low tone.

"Mr. Schmalzried, you have a five-pound six-ounce baby girl and your wife is just fine."

"Great, Doctor, just what Maureen, our daughter, wanted—a sister," I replied happily.

"But all is not well with the baby. She has two toes grown together." He then cleared his throat.

I felt the doctor was observing my reactions as he tested my emotional strength. "Gosh, Doctor," I replied, "that's nothing to worry about. Surely a few toes can be separated."

The doctor smiled briefly for the first time and then said, "Yes, the toes can be separated if necessary by surgical operation, but this is not our biggest problem." He was still watching me very closely and evidently decided to continue and tell me the worst. "I want you to keep in mind that my diagnosis is not definite, but your baby is a—'mongoloid.' "

"Mongoloid, what is that, Doctor?"

He explained, "The term mongoloid* is a name given to babies having some features of the Mongolian race, such as the inward slant of their eyes. Other characteristics are common: The hair is stringy or silky, and the head is usually small and round. The tongue is furrowed and coarse. The fifth or little finger is short and tends to curve inward. The mongoloid child is also mentally and physically retarded, seldom reaching the mentality of a seven or eight-year-old child; physical achievements are slow. This may come to you as a shock, but you are not alone with this problem—there are probably eighty thousand mongoloids in the United States."

---

*Since this story was originally written, all children thus born are diagnosed as having a genetic defect termed "Down's Syndrome."

My mind was wandering, and I didn't think to ask any questions. The doctor, patting me lightly on the back, said, "Please don't tell your wife about this. I delivered the baby and feel it is my responsibility to break this news to her at the opportune time."

To this request I wholeheartedly agreed. The doctor, satisfied with the way I accepted the bad news, shook my hand and said, "If I can be of any further help, just let me know. I also want to thank you for placing so much confidence in me. You may now see your wife—she is in Room 220." He turned and left, and it seemed as if something of myself left with him. However, I did not comprehend the seriousness of the situation. "Surely," I thought, "Doctor Altdoerffer must be mistaken, as we couldn't possibly have a retarded baby—oh, dear merciful God, not us!"

I lost no time in running up the stairs to the second floor. Room 220 may have been buzzing with activity earlier, but now the shades were drawn and all was quiet. My beloved Alice was still groggy and sleepy. As I looked down at her, she appeared extraordinarily beautiful in spite of the fact that she was enveloped in one of those unsightly, oversized, white hospital gowns. As I continued to look at her I remembered the lines of Shakespeare—"She is mine own; and I am rich in having such a jewel, as twenty seas if all their sands were pearls, the water nectar, and the rocks pure gold." I stayed in the room for a short time listening to Alice's senseless, semi-conscious chatter. When she dozed again into a deep sleep, I gently kissed her on her forehead and softly whispered, "Pleasant dreams and goodbye until tonight."

Home

Alice's mother, Margaret Geis, was a kind, loving person. She believed that the luxury of doing good works for others superseded every other personal enjoyment. With these fine qualities, how could I but help being proud to call her, "Mother"? During our present emergency she again volunteered to help take care of the children. Taking care of a large home with five growing grandchildren is quite a task, and, not wanting to take advantage of her kindness, I hurried home to give this wonderful person a breather from the difficult chores.

Everybody rushed to the living room as I opened the front door. They were all excited and wanted to know if Mom was all right and if God had given them a brother or sister. They were happy to learn that their mother was just fine. Bernie and Maureen were especially thrilled about having a sister. The smaller boys just said, "aw" and went back to playing Cowboys and Indians. I said nothing of the bad news that burned in my heart.

Back to Hospital Again P.M.

That evening Alice was wide awake and alert. She was glad to see me, and we both laughed when she accused me of being one minute late as she pointed to the hands on her wristwatch. She was thrilled when she told me that she had held the baby for a brief time. "Oh, Honey, you will love the baby," Alice said so happily. "She is the sweetest little thing that God ever made; she is a little *sunshine* and the only

baby we ever had that looks so much like me." I smiled and said nothing. In the midst of her happiness she sensed that something was wrong. She asked me why the baby had to be in an incubator, why it looked so blue under the eyes, why she was not permitted to hold the baby for longer periods of time. These questions placed me in an uncomfortable position. I didn't know just how to answer them without possibly jeopardizing her recovery. I either evaded the questions or answered them very vaguely. Finally, I managed to change the subject and started a nice conversation about our other children, which was good for Alice, for as St. Augustine once said, "What tigress is there that does not purr over her young ones, and fawn upon them in tenderness?" We were enjoying ourselves so much that I lost all notion of the time, that is, until a nurse quite dutifully reminded me visiting hours were over.

May 30th

I always enjoyed taking the children to see the parade with its many colorful bands keeping in step with the rhythmic marching music, the sounding of the taps—which always brings tears to my eyes—and the sharp crack of rifles firing a volley of shots over our heroes' graves. But this Memorial Day morning was different, and the celebration could not hold my interest. My thoughts were only with Alice at the North Side Hospital. For the children's sake, however, I tried to appear cheerful and happy, and I do believe my camouflaged enthusiasm was not detected by my little merry companions. I was tormented with the thought that at this very moment the doctor might be breaking the news to her about the baby. How would she accept the news? Would she become hysterical? I didn't know. This was the very first time that we were faced with tragic news in our fifteen years of married life, and I therefore could not measure her emotional reactions on any past experience. I was tortured with the desire to be at her side at this very moment, but felt so utterly helpless and powerless, because I could not be with her until visiting hours in the afternoon. It has been said that every moment of time is more valuable than every thread of gold. This may be true, but on that morning, time had no value to me. I wanted to be with Alice so much, to console her, to wipe away her tears, that I would gladly have traded the minutes for hours if this would have sped the hands of the clock to point to 2 P.M.

Visiting Hours—2:00 P.M.

In my eagerness to get to the hospital I arrived forty-five minutes early. Since visiting hours were strictly enforced in this hospital, there wasn't anything I could do but wait. I sat in a comfortable chair in the lobby, twiddling my thumbs and thinking how foolish it was for me to leave the house so early, when I had so many household chores to do. Helping with the housework made me appreciate Alice all the more. I began to realize how true the saying, "Man's work is from dawn to dusk, but a woman's work is never done." Also, while trying to be a mother, I saw how important are those little things that a mother does for her children, which, though we notice, we take for granted and fail to see, in each deed of discipline or love, the building of a strong character in the child.

Time, with all its clarity, moves slowly for him whose whole employment is to watch its flight. Thanks to my daydreaming, this did not happen to me. Those forty-five minutes fled swiftly. It was now two o'clock, time for all new fathers to throw out their chests, make goo-goo eyes and other comical gestures as they peek through the nursery window at their future Presidents, Miss Americas, and baseball stars. For me, however, it was a straight path to Alice. She looked wonderful, more like a Miss Universe than a new mother. She was so cheerful it was amazing, and I was at first dubious that the doctor had even told her about the baby. However, she told me the doctor had been in to see her shortly before noon and told her all about the condition of the baby. Alice then told me that she was not surprised as she suspected something was wrong. What concerned her the most was not our littlest one, herself, or me. Her deepest anxiety was for our daughter, Maureen.

"Oh, Bern! How will Maureen accept a retarded sister?" She hesitated, then after a moment continued, "Maureen wanted a sister so much. Have I let her down?"

I came a little closer and said, "Don't worry about Maureen. Besides, the doctor said he may be wrong, so let's wait and see."

"No, Bern, the doctor said she gives every evidence of being a mongoloid. I am glad he was so honest with us. Now we know what to expect, and it's so much better to know now than to find out later."

But still holding on to the long odds, I replied, "I talked this over with a friend of mine

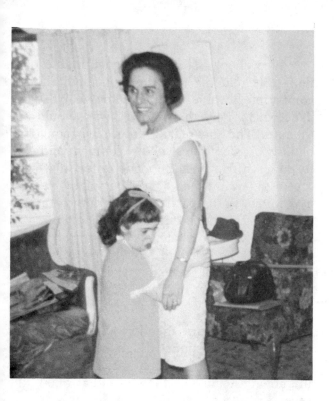

whose wife is a nurse, and he told me she said
many of these babies turn out to be geniuses."

Alice smiled at my grasping for hope. "Darling, we should accept the facts that the doctor
gave us. If she develops into a genius—good; if
not, we won't be further hurt or disappointed."

Alice's reasoning made good sense, but I
didn't want to believe it. I then lied, "I believe
you're right," and patted her on the hand. "Did
the doctor tell you anything more about the
baby?"

Alice changed to a more comfortable position. "He told me that the mongoloid child is compatible, lovable, and never known to become dangerous. For this alone, we should be thankful. The only real difference in a mongoloid child is his slow physical development and ability to learn. He must be made to feel that he is loved and wanted as a member of the family. You know, Bern, my heart went out to our doctor today. He choked up with emotion when he said, 'Mrs. Schmalzried, take this baby home and give her all the love and care you possibly can. I am sure you will never regret it. Remember if you have room in your heart you will find room in your house.' "

"Did the doctor mention what caused this condition?" I questioned. "Yes, he said there are many theories, but the definite cause is unknown. A current theory is that about the second month after conception oxygen was temporarily shut off to the baby for some reason.* He assured me that sometimes these births happen and the parents are not in any way responsible. He also told me that heredity is not a determining factor."

---

*Since the date of this story, Doctors Jerome Lejeune and Raymond Turpin, of the *Institut de Progenes Forulte de Medecine,* Paris, demonstrated that mongolism is a genetic defect. Victims are all born with 47 chromosomes in their cells instead of the normal 46.

Maureen and Sunshine

From Alice's cheerful attitude it was obvious that the doctor had explained everything in such a way that Alice accepted the facts, and, surprisingly to me, accepted the child for what she was—her baby.

Then she happily told me that our pastor, Father Norman Kelly, had been in to see her. "Oh Bern, he was so nice and consoling. He told me this baby may be our means of getting to heaven." She then told me that she suggested to Father that the baby be baptized, and Father told her this already had been done. "Yes, darling," I interrupted, "Doctor Altdoerffer advised me to have it done as soon as possible as the baby's physical condition was 'touch and go.' Yesterday, as soon as I left the hospital, I called the parish house, and Father David Lettau, assistant pastor, rushed to the hospital and baptized the baby."

At the end of visiting hours as I bent over to kiss Alice, she asked me not to tell Maureen. She wanted to call her on the telephone and explain the news to her in a more tender, understanding, motherly fashion. I don't know what magic words Alice used in explaining the baby's condition to our nine-year-old daughter, but it was amazing when I later learned she commented, "Even a retarded sister is better than none."

Facing the Facts

I left the hospital feeling things were a little better. Alice had accepted the news about the baby with a mother's heart. I still felt that the doctor was mistaken and that the baby as she grew older would develop into a healthy, normal child. Relaxed, I drove towards home—thankful, cheerful and humming the tunes coming from the car radio. I didn't have a care in the world—at least right now.

Then it happened, like a bolt of lightning out of a clear sky—I could not shake from my mind the thought that the baby was retarded. I would only be a fool to cling to the hope that the doctor made a mistake—he was too good a doctor. I tried my best to put these thoughts away, but reason gave way to the frantic fears of imagination. I visualized alarming, ugly things. I could see my retarded daughter as the target of mockery by other children. I saw the devastating effects it would have on my other children—they would be marked, ashamed to bring their friends home. These things and a million more I can't recall sped before my mind's eye. Then, trying to brighten this dismal picture, I thought surely there must be someone, somewhere, to whom we could turn for hope. Then I remembered the doctor saying how futile it would be to rush into the hallowed halls of specialists in a frantic search for a cure. There is no cure for mongolism. If there were, all doctors would be aware of it.

I was confused, depressed, and shocked. It's not fair for God to create such children. Why should He punish Alice and me by sending us a mongoloid baby? I was in no mood to go home and face the children; I was distraught and at loose ends with myself. I needed someone to talk to, someone who understood. But who? I wasn't looking for sympathy—I just wanted to talk with somebody. St. Christopher did a good job of protecting me as I drove around the town aimlessly. My mind was more on my problems than on the road. I finally decided to visit the one Person who could help me. I drove to my parish church of St. Rose. At this time of day the church was empty. The flickering red flames of the vigil light reminded me, however, that indeed I was not alone. This is the way I had hoped it to be. I knelt in a front pew and prayed to our divine Lord present in the tabernacle.

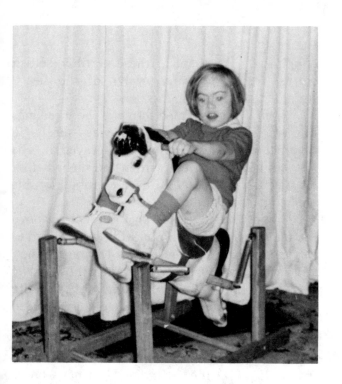

I talked to Him from the depths of my heart. I had never spoken to Him like this before—I told Him my problems and spared no words in describing my feelings—I was hurt and I told Him so....

"Oh God, why did You do this to Alice and me? What have we done to deserve such a cross? It isn't fair for You to do this horrible thing to us.... Please, please, Lord," I cried, "don't punish us this way. It would be so easy for You to call this infant back to Your heavenly home and allow me and my family to live in peace and happiness." As I spoke these terribly selfish words, tears, the safety valve of the heart, streamed down my cheeks.

Should I be ashamed to make these feelings known? God knew how weak I was—surely He understood. Had not our Lord prayed to His heavenly Father in the garden the night before He died on the cross, "If it be possible, let this chalice pass from me"?

I then fixed my eyes on the crucifix above the tabernacle. The limp, pitiful figure nailed to the cross reminded me of His terrible passion and death. I don't know for certain how long I stared in a trancelike gaze meditating on the life of Jesus, but when I finally walked out of church my emotions were under control, and I was more composed. I assume just talking and unloading my troubles on Someone's shoulders bolstered my morale. On the other hand, perhaps I was just pleased with myself for coming to God so early rather than waiting until the eleventh hour, or when all other avenues of hope were exhausted. However, this visit did not solve all my problems. I was still reluctant to accept a baby who would not be capable of developing into a good student, a successful business woman, or a loving mother.

In spite of my feelings I realized the more knowledge I had regarding the subject of retardation, the better equipped I would be to face problems realistically. Therefore, instead of going straight home from church, I changed direction and headed for the Catholic Book and Film Center operated by the Daughters of St. Paul. There I purchased a very helpful book on retarded children. The author of this book had many years of experience with retarded children. In it she shares her findings, philosophy, and hopes for the future regarding the education and care of these special children of God.

The facts in print were exactly as my doctor had explained them to me. However, the book was more thorough, covering just about everything one would wish to know about these children. This definitely erased several ugly ideas I had already formed about retarded children, making the picture not nearly as black as it had seemed at first.

Family United

The day Alice came home from the hospital was a great event. All were thankful and thrilled to see Mommy take her rightful place as queen of the home. She unquestionably is the rallying-point around which affection and obedience develop. But the day was saddened with the thought that we had to leave the baby in the hospital for a few days longer.

The Family Circle—left to right: Sunshine, Mommy, Robert, Bernie, Pop, Maureen, Albert, and James

Then the baby came home. She was very delicate and required extra special handling and care. She had difficulty in swallowing the formula and trouble retaining the milk. This condition contributed to her slow gain in weight and further added to her very slow physical development. Her achievements were extremely slow, but, of course, this was no surprise to us as we were well advised as to her needs.

Alice and the children accepted the baby— she was one of the family. I could understand the children's attitude as their young minds were not mature enough to realize the full impact of the seriousness of mental retardation.

Alice's joyous acceptance was puzzling to me. It was far beyond even the duties of a mother's love, I thought. Surely I loved the little tot in a way—after all, I was her father, and besides she was so frail and so dependent on all of us. How could I refuse such a helpless little creature my care and love? To do otherwise would not be human. If I refused my love to my own flesh and blood, could I have the audacity to say to my God, "I love You!"?

Though my heart was heavy, I kept my sadness and disappointment locked within me. I didn't want my feelings to become contagious and afflict the other members of my family, who were so happy with the baby. To hide my true sentiments, I forcibly developed a contented, merry attitude, treating her as if nothing was wrong.

I was surprised when I read in the book how some parents mistakenly feel ashamed and consider giving birth to a handicapped child as a punishment or chastisement. This thought had never entered my mind. Perhaps I was spared this added mental anguish since I had turned to God so early in my troubles. I also felt if we tried to keep the baby's condition a secret, we would only arouse suspicion, so we spoke freely about it. This proved most beneficial, particularly for the children, and as a result they were not the least bit embarrassed to bring their playmates home to see their little sister.

Telling the Children

We did not delay in telling the children what to expect of their new baby sister. We simply and briefly explained that almighty God in His all-wise plan had kept a part of their little sister's intellect or mental powers in heaven; just as He might keep the part of the body of some other little babies, such as their eyes, hearing, hands, in heaven, awaiting the day of the glorious resurrection of the body, so too He had done this for **their little sister.**

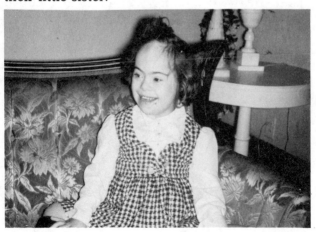

We told them they must be kind, consider-
ate, and helpful to their little sister. They were to
watch over her. We described the role of the
Guardian Angel and explained that they were
also to be like guardian angels to their little handicapped sister. In this way the children received
a truthful explanation and an inspiration for their
mode of conduct. They were instilled with a
sense of responsibility and learned to recognize
what their retarded sister was capable of doing
and not doing. Thus all members of the family
contributed to the guardianship and training of
their special sister.

When the children noticed something was
wrong and asked what it was, we told them the
truth immediately in a way they would understand. In the beginning we informed them to
the extent we felt best for them and for their
little sister; beyond that, we waited for their
questions.

"A Ray of Sunshine"

As the baby grew a little older she became more animated and noticed objects. She started to do things, like follow my finger with her eyes, or grasp her rattle. Each new accomplishment was a thrill, and each of us, including myself, took pride in being the first to notice a new achievement. We would boast to our friends of her progress at six months the way people ordinarily proudly speak of their children at one month.

Not to love this baby would have been impossible. She possessed a personality that diffused happiness. I believe this magical quality, this dynamism, is a special gift to her from God. Because of her deficiency in one thing, God in His wisdom bestowed upon her something else. He gave to our Mary Margaret this extraordinary quality that generated joy and love. In our own home, the powers of this child's ability to evoke love and happiness were indescribable. Even I

was thawing under its influence and could no longer resist the urge to accept the appropriate pet name the rest of the family had given her—"Sunshine." Alice had first used this name in the hospital when she held the baby in her arms for the very first time.

With the passing of each day I grew to love "Sunshine" more and more. She was truly a little ray of sunshine. Many times after a grueling day at the office, like we all experience occasionally, holding her in my arms would change the whole gloomy world into a land of sunshine. Even so, in spite of this, I could not entirely accept her retarded condition. Worried by my attitude, I looked upon myself as a Jekyll and Hyde, or like a new car without a motor—shiny on the outside but oh, so empty on the inside. I eased my conscience: Could I not love my child as a person, yet resent her condition? At times I would look into her beautiful blue eyes and the materialistic thought, "What a waste of God's creative powers," tortured me, as if seven lances were piercing my heart.

Prayer for a Miracle

Finally, I conceived the idea of a miracle. "Why didn't I think of this before? Could it be that is what God wants me to do—pray for a

At the shrine of St. Anne de Beaupre, Canada—Maureen, Mommy, Sunshine

miracle? The Bible tells us many stories of people being restored to health by Jesus, and even today God still occasionally manifests His powers by working physical miracles for persons with hopeless physical conditions. With these thoughts in mind I prayed with a new motivation, new vigor, and renewed hope. Yes, I prayed for a miracle, and why not? Did not God say, "Ask and you shall receive"? I certainly asked, but after nursing the baby through the long winter, my prayer was not answered.

But I never stopped praying or became discouraged. I was sure that if I prayed enough, God could not refuse my request. So I bombarded heaven with prayers and more prayers—and not from a book, but from my heart. At last the answer came, although at the time I did not realize it.

Mary's Mother

I took the whole family on a journey eight hundred miles to St. Anne de Beaupre, Quebec, Canada, the shrine of the mother of Mary, the Mother of God. Why I happened to think of this shrine, or even St. Anne, was a mystery to me. It must have been heaven answering my prayers, because, although I had often heard people speak of this shrine, I was never interested enough to inquire about it, or to bother reading about its history. In fact, I am ashamed to confess that I never even knew who St. Anne was. I had never associated her with the mother of the Virgin Mary. I feel that God realized I needed a consoling friend, one who would understand, one who could give me courage, strength, and, above all, a stronger faith. He then placed me in the custody of St. Anne for the spiritual guidance I needed so badly.

Planning the Trip

This was 1957, and our 1951 model automobile was not very roomy, especially for all of us to be cramped in at the same time. College boys cramming phone booths had nothing on us. How would we survive an eight hundred mile trip when just an eighty mile jaunt to Pittsburgh, Pennsylvania, was quite a task. I realized the weather conditions would play an important role as I cannot think of a condition more uncomfortable than riding in a crowded car on a long trip, on a sweltering day, with a half-dozen energetic children.

Another concern was whether our recently acquired, used, six-year-old automobile would make the trip without any serious breakdown. Worrying ceased when I concluded that, "If St. Anne wants us to get to her shrine, she will see to it that the car holds together."

On Our Way

The last Friday in June, 1957, we visited Alice's parents at their summer cottage on Canadahta Lake, near Union City, Pa. This resort was directly on our route to Canada. Stopping here, after a good eighty mile start, offered a weekend of relaxation—boating, fishing, and swimming—before starting our long trip.

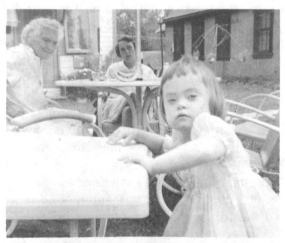

Grandma Geis, Mommy and Sunshine—Canadahta Lake, Pennsylvania

On the following Monday morning, after participating in the Holy Sacrifice of the Mass and receiving Holy Communion at St. Teresa's Church in Union City, Pa., we were on our way.

The day turned out to be a perfect one for traveling. I was so pleased with the change in the weather (up to now it had been extremely hot) that I could only believe that St. Anne had sympathetically arranged it. It was a bright day, yet cloudy enough to shade us from the burning sun. Occasionally it rained just enough to keep the highway cool without causing unfavorable driving conditions.

In addition to the ideal weather, the children, crowded as they were, never behaved better. The miles ticked off rather pleasantly and the time went quickly. Periodically we would stop to stretch our cramped legs and refresh ourselves with a soft drink.

We left the New York Thruway at North Syracuse, New York, and headed north on Route 11. The route so far had not been very scenic, but we were making good time, much better than I had anticipated. It was about 5 P.M. when we decided to stop for the night at Adams Center, N.Y., almost half-way to our destination.

My fatigue gave way to welcome sleep, which restored me for another busy day. Our second day began again by attending Holy Mass at nearby St. Cecilia's Church. It gave me a sense of pride to attend Mass with my entire family, and especially to kneel at the Communion railing with my wife, daughter Maureen, and two sons, Bernie and Robert. As I waited for the priest to place the Sacred Host in my mouth, I recalled the happenings of the Last Supper as told by St. Luke 22:27.... "And having taken bread, He gave thanks and broke, and gave it to them, saying 'This is my body, which is being given for you. Do this in remembrance of me.'" As the priest administered the Host to each of us, he said, "Corpus Christi" (The Body of Christ).... And as he stood before me and spoke these words, I knew my time of waiting was over, my hope was now a reality as I received the greatest Gift of my Faith and God's love. Could there be any doubt as to why I was proud to kneel with my family to receive the Body of Christ? I was also looking forward to the day when Albert and James reached their seventh birthdays, so they, too, could kneel with us to receive the Bread of Life.

After a light breakfast, we again headed towards Canada. We were happy to know that if we made as much progress as we had the day before we would be at St. Anne's by nightfall. After a few hours driving we were tempted to take a scenic boat ride around the Thousand Islands. However, as inviting and interesting as the signboard appeals seemed to be, we decided against it as it would consume too much time. Our prime objective was to reach St. Anne's with as little delay as possible. In fact, with so many children in the car we had our normal, "I have to," stops.

It was noon when we passed over the border into Canada. For the children, knowing they were in a foreign country was an added thrill. Soon we were driving through the great city of Montreal. I assume there are many things of interest in this great industrial Canadian city, but, again, we spared no time for sight-seeing.

The trip began to take on new interest. It was amusing for the children to hear people speak in a different language, and they found it very amusing to see me trying to communicate with the French Canadians with my hands. They began to record a French vocabulary with their pads and pencils as many signs were written in French with the English translation. And so education and interest kept restless bodies in tow.

Lady of the Cape

Trois Rivieres was our next stop. A friend of mine told me I must stop at the Shrine of the Lady of the Cape, and I intended to take his advice. We were most impressed with the shrine and the history of Cape de la Madeleine and its founding. In fact, we found it so impressive that the time sped by much faster than we had anticipated. Beaupre was only about one hundred miles to the north, so we decided, rather than risk traveling at night, we would stay at Trois Rivieres. By making this decision we could take part in the colorful candlelight procession and other impressive evening devotions at Cape de la Madeleine. Although we were now slightly behind schedule, we had no regrets, for the time we spent at this shrine was a memorable one. It came at a time when our bodies were tired from traveling; and St. Anne, the wise, loving person that she is, directed us to this shrine of her daughter, Mary, for both physical and spiritual renewal.

The next morning the church was so crowded for eight o'clock Mass, we wondered from where all the people had come. As we left the church it began to drizzle. However, it was only a shower, and the sun was still shining. This combination of rain and sun resulted in the most beautiful rainbow I had ever seen. As I looked at this arch of beautiful colors stretching across the St. Lawrence River, I wanted to believe it was St. Anne's way of expressing her satisfaction with us for spending some time at her daughter's shrine.

Safe Arrival

We reached "Old" Quebec before noon on Wednesday. This was where the British, under General Wolfe, scaled the high cliffs, surprised, and defeated the French under General Montcalm, in the battle known as the Abraham Plains. Little did I realize as I read my history book in school that some day I would be passing through this historical city on my way to Beaupre seeking a miracle. After leaving the city of Quebec, we still had twenty miles to travel before reaching our destination.

We were excited and anxious—so anxious to reach our goal that the children became unusually quiet as they were concentrating and focusing their eyes on the highway far ahead, each wanting to be the very first one to see the famous shrine. Those twenty miles, because of our anxiety, seemed to go exceedingly slow. This was all a matter of mind as we arrived in very good time.

We first saw the towers of the Basilica about two miles in the distance. At this moment the silence was broken instantaneously by everyone excitedly shouting in one big loud happy chorus —"There's St. Anne's."

Along the way we had momentarily mistaken other churches for the shrine. But the one we were now approaching, off to our left, was unmistakably the Shrine of St. Anne. The two unfinished towers, without steeples, reaching for the heavens, looked exactly like the many photographs we had seen so many times before.

I said a silent prayer of thanksgiving for the excellent way the baby endured the long ride, for the safe protection of all of us, and for the fine traveling weather, also for the fine behavior and consideration for one another that contributed so much to the pleasure of the trip.

Our first duty and objective was to find a place to stay and take care of our weary bodies. We had no trouble in finding a very nice motel within walking distance of the Basilica. After unpacking the luggage and eating lunch, we were now ready and eager to take the baby to the "Land of Miracles."

St. Anne's Basilica

There are, no doubt, bigger churches in the world, but to me this was the largest. When I stepped inside, it was even more spacious than I had imagined. The length is three hundred seventy-five feet. Two thousand persons can be seated, while eight thousand more may stand in the transept and in the large ambulatories. The Basilica has been under construction since 1923, and there is still work to be done before it is entirely completed.

As we walked with awe into this vast marvel of architecture, we saw crutches, braces, and many other physical aids that the cured had left in the Basilica as evidence of good St. Anne's intercession. We continued slowly and reverently up the center aisle towards the main altar. The architect, L. N. Sherbrooke, P.Q., must have had the throne of God in mind when he designed this altar with its magnificent surroundings. The altar is partly surrounded by gigantic white marble columns, which support the large dome. At the top of the dome is a large painting of the Child Jesus, Mary, and St. Anne. I enjoyed looking at this painting, for it was a reminder to me that the Holy Family was happily looking down at my family this very moment, welcoming us to this "Land of Miracles."

"What a model God has given to us in this Holy Family!" I thought.

We knelt in a front pew and paid our respects to our divine Lord, present in the tabernacle. Then we proceeded towards the miraculous statue of St. Anne. Many people were kneeling, others standing; also mingled in the crowd were the crippled and sick, who, like us, came to St. Anne's shrine in North America, seeking her help.

The miraculous statue of St. Anne is very beautiful. It has been rightly said that the face as shown in this image expresses the kindness of a mother and the dignity of a queen. On her right arm she holds the infant Mary. Her left hand points to heaven—the source of the power she shares with her daughter, and at her feet are countless crutches, representing tangible evidence of this power. She wears the brilliant diadem with which she was crowned when Pope Leo XIII proclaimed her patroness of Quebec, and she is surrounded by the golden rays which are symbolic of her glory in heaven.

For the past month I had rehearsed what I intended to say when this moment arrived.

"Good St. Anne," I would beg, "please, please go before the Throne of God and plead with Him to cure our baby!"

Surprisingly, however, when I actually stood looking at the face of St. Anne, I could not bring myself to ask for a miracle. Instead I found myself thanking God for all the blessings He had bestowed upon me and my family—and most particularly for our Catholic Faith.

During the first twenty-four hours we spent as much time as possible in the Basilica. The baby was blessed by the priest, and we all had the privilege of kissing the major relic, a large wristbone of St. Anne. We prayed at numerous chapels and before the relics of various saints. We drank from the miraculous fountain. We made the Stations of the Cross on the hillside, and on our knees made the torturous twenty-eight steps.

Historical Quebec

At noon on our second day we decided to go into Old Quebec and do a little sightseeing. I was always one who liked history and enjoyed visiting places where history was made. We saw the enclosure wall, the City Gates, the Citadel, the Battlefield Park where England had won the battle for Canada, and other historical places. Surprisingly to me, none of these historical places held my interest. All I had in mind was getting back to the shrine.

My visit to Old Quebec was not a complete loss. Our children are taught by the Ursuline nuns so I thought it would be interesting to visit the Ursuline Convent. Having been built in 1639, it is the most ancient one in Canada. At the convent we had the honor of talking to the Mother Superior, Mother St. George, a member of the order for forty-nine years. She related how she was privileged to actually witness two physical cures at Beaupre before she became a nun. The details of her story made me all the more anxious to get back to the shrine and ask for a miracle. After all was this not the reason we had come to Beaupre?

Asking for a Cure

Early evening found us back at the shrine. Bernie, Jr., our oldest boy, carried the baby, and soon we stood again under the miraculous statue. This time I was definitely pleading for a miracle. Perhaps the others were, too.

All of a sudden the baby gave a quick jerk, almost jumping out of Bernie's gentle, but firm grasp. At the same time, she lifted her little head slightly and smiled. We all noticed this strange incident—it was so pronounced. We could see the surprised look on Bernie's face and the tightening of his embrace. Later he said he thought the baby was going to jump out of his arms.

This was most unusual. The baby was so delicate and limp. Even though she was more than a year old, she had never been known to stiffen her body, and her neck was so weak she never had the strength to raise her head without the help of somebody supporting it.

We will never know what really happened at that moment. Could it be, I asked myself, that St. Anne made herself visible to Mary Margaret, and perhaps even kissed her on the cheek and said a few encouraging words to her?

Home Again

We stayed until noon of the third day and then started our long ride for Girard, Ohio. When we arrived home we did not forget Saint Anne. Rather, in a manner of speaking, we brought her home with us. Even though our long trip did not seem to have accomplished its purpose, we gained a great affection and love for St. Anne. She seemed to be a member of our family now—our adopted heavenly Grandmother.

I was only momentarily disappointed because God did not work a miracle. This only made me blame myself and prompted me to take inventory. Perhaps I was too unworthy in the sight of God to receive such a favor. "Could it be," I asked myself, "that I have been trying to win favor with God on my own terms?"

Have I unintentionally fallen into a slothful attitude in regard to my spiritual life? This is a real possibility, because in this troubled and busy world I seem to have so little time to spend on the cultivation of my spiritual life. True, I worship God on Sundays and faithfully say my morning and evening prayers, prayers at meals, sometimes attend Mass during the week, and even say a few little extra prayers during the day. But, this all is done, for the most part, through routine, or at my own convenience. Is this all my religion should mean to me; why don't I allow it to mean more to me? Have I unconsciously permitted myself to consider God a myth, or a God who does nothing, a God I don't need? No! I don't really believe so. I know everything we do, everything we have, every beat of our heart, the rising of the sun, the stability of the entire universe, depends on the controlling hands of God. God is the vine, we are only the branches —without Him we can do nothing. Perhaps I have been guilty of taking God "for granted," giving Him no thanks for all my blessings, and showing Him no sincere love. How could I go on accepting all the fruits of life, both spiritual and material, without acknowledging to God my sincere appreciation and deep, true love?

After taking inventory I came to these conclusions: A few extra prayers when I found the time was surely insufficient proof of my love. I must do more that requires sacrifice, because virtue cultivated through sacrifice runs truer and deeper. If I were to attain an ever closer friendship with God my actions must express and intensify my inner force of love, for nothing worth having is ever achieved without striving. I now realized if I wished to be a friend of God I must act like a friend. I must prove my love with my actions. So many times in the past I had failed because I thought only of doing big things, always putting off the little ones. The realization now came that the small sacrifices are so important, that if we do not first attempt these the danger prevails of never making the start on the big ones.

I then decided to make an honest effort to attend daily Mass and receive Holy Communion frequently. Rising a bit earlier each morning would not entail too much extra effort although walking to church in all kinds of weather might require a little sacrifice. My thoughts then turned to God's real Presence in the tabernacle. If I really believed in this Mystery of Faith, and I most certainly did, then why was it I walked past the House of God so many times without even thinking of stopping for a visit? I wouldn't walk past a friend's house without at least stopping to say hello. This line of reasoning made sound logic to me. I, therefore, promptly made up my mind to make more visits to church, regardless of how brief they might be. Another determined decision was to make a "Closed Weekend Retreat." I had often been invited to make a retreat and agreed that it would be most beneficial, but I could never spare one of my precious weekends for God. I was forever going to the lake, to the ball park, just too busy one way or another. Oh, how flimsy were these excuses, my dear God, how foolish of me!

As time went on I persevered in my intentions of attending daily Mass and receiving Holy Communion frequently. I also found time and formed the comforting habit of stopping in church every day immediately after work. These brief visits, requiring little effort or sacrifice, made me feel so good, for I had the feeling they were so much appreciated. Can you imagine God, the Creator of all the universe, appreciating visits from me! Yet, in His majestic humility, He is there waiting for us always.

I also made my first weekend retreat at the Sacred Heart Retreat House. During the forty hours on retreat, away from the hustle and bustle of the busy world, I really learned to know God better and consequently began to love Him more. I found myself practicing my religion not only more ardently, but with greater joy as it took on new meaning with each effort to apply it to daily living.

It became evident to me that through my baby, my faith had grown stronger, my knowledge and understanding of God fuller, and my desire to requite His love more intense. However, I mistakenly thought that because of this spiritual uplift God owed me something and that He would surely reward my sincerity of purpose by performing a miracle, and with this in mind I planned a second family pilgrimage to St. Anne's.

Seriously Sick

Whatever early plans I had made about our second visit to St. Anne's became very shaky in February.

One evening when Alice tucked the baby into her crib, she was perfectly well, no noticeable signs of any illness.

It was about 10 P.M. when we heard the baby gasping for breath. We rushed her to the emergency room of St. Elizabeth's Hospital, and Doctor Louis Zeller, our family physician, admitted her at once. She was given medication and shots of the wonder drugs, and placed in oxygen. The doctor did not give us much encouragement and asked for permission to perform a tracheotomy, if necessary, to ease her breathing.

This developed into a night of agony, a night of prayer. I didn't want anything to happen to this baby. I was frightened now when I recalled that not too long ago I had pleaded with God to call this little creature back to His heavenly home. I guess God was now teaching me another lesson that we should not be too impulsive when we ask Him for favors. So many times we ask for things that are not always good for us. But, I pleaded, "Dear God, please let us keep our baby, please, at least for a little while longer!"

The next day she showed some improvement. The throat incision was not necessary, and she continued to respond favorably to treatment. On the third day the oxygen was discontinued.

The fifth day, to the surprise of everyone, she was released from the hospital. Everybody was amazed at her speedy, complete recovery. A friend of ours, a nurse on the floor, now told us that when "Sunshine" was admitted, she was pessimistic about her survival. There were others who thought if she did recover, that she would be in the hospital for a long time.

Before Mary Margaret left the hospital she found a tender spot in the hearts of all who came in contact with her. It was so obvious when nurses and visitors alike gathered around her crib, their faces beamed with happy smiles, as if this little baby was the sunlight the Lord sent to brighten their day.

Mrs. Rose Serbian, who for six years had worked on the pediatrics floor, had this to say about Mary Margaret. "All children are sweet and lovable, but your little darling, besides these usual qualities, has a little more. She is special; something about her is extraordinary. I studied her, trying to figure what it was that gave her such a dynamic personality. I finally came to the conclusion that it was her smile. She has one of the sweetest, most radiant, warmest smiles I have ever seen, one that I think even the angels might envy."

This description fitted Mary Margaret perfectly. I never have seen her frown—I guess she doesn't know how. Her smile is to people what the sunshine is to flowers. And, as she scatters her smiles along life's pathways, the good she will do is inconceivable. There is no better tonic than a smile to lighten the burdens of illness, poverty, and affliction; it converts ignorance into an amiable simplicity and gives encouragement to the depressed.

Second Trip to St. Anne's

It had been exactly twelve months earlier when we made our first visit to St. Anne's Shrine. This, our second trip, was similar to the first, with only slight variation. One of these changes was to visit St. Joseph's Shrine of Mount Royal, in Montreal. It is estimated that over 2,000,000 pilgrims and visitors flock to this shrine each year. To visit the Oratory of St. Joseph's was not far off our route, and therefore we did not really lose much traveling time. We arrived at St. Anne's again on a Wednesday and stayed again until Friday. As we left the shrine for the second time our prayers once again were not answered. At least that is what I thought as I turned out of the parking lot at the Basilica, but just then, a station wagon with California license tags pulled into my vacated space. This car was a new model, but was aged-looking from the dirt and grime accumulated during the many miles of travel. Inside were cramped a half dozen children, the little ones each showing all over their tiny faces evidence that they had recently eaten chocolate bars. They were an energetic lot, climbing over luggage and one another, each battling to gain a vantage point by the window for a better view of the Basilica. The parents, however, were pitiful looking. They were worn out by parent responsibility and the long, tiresome ride; they were physically exhausted, and they showed it. There was no smile, no excited emotions, just a fixed, expressionless, weary stare. A mannequin almost appeared more lifelike than these tired parents. I would have felt sorry for them if I had not known from my own personal experience that for whatever reasons they chose to journey over three thousand miles in a crowded automobile, St. Anne would surely appreciate it and love them most dearly for all their sacrifices. She would take their pleas to the throne of God, and He in turn would shower them abundantly with His graces and blessings.

Back Home

On the journey home, I had a lot of time to recall the many things that took place during our three-day stay at the shrine. The most impressive sight, the one I could not shake from my mind, was the invalids. They were of all ages: young, old and in-between. They were on crutches, in wheelchairs, and on stretchers. From talking with their companions who accompanied them on their long trip, I learned that the afflicted, although in pain, never uttered a word of complaint while traveling. No wonder it has been said that God must draw His best soldiers from the ranks of the suffering. It was evident from their expressions that they were not despairing, but rather filled with hope and consolation. It amazed me to see one with a pitiful, broken, bent body smile and extend a light pat of encouragement to a cripple whom he thought needed relief more than himself.

"Lay up for yourselves treasures in heaven, where neither rust nor moth consumes, nor thieves break in and steal." This is what the afflicted must have seen as their tears of sorrow turned into telescopes bringing God's love so close to them. How else could they so willingly accept their sufferings, and with such a strong will to bear them?

Then I thought of the loved ones of these afflicted who so unselfishly gave their time to bring them on this pilgrimage of hope. I believe, at least for most people, it is more painful to have a loved one ill than it is for the afflicted person himself. The sacrifice required for perpetual, around-the-clock nursing care is none other than true love in action. These people in their charity and love do not speculate on their duty, but simply do it. When they have done it, however blindly, perhaps someday God will show them why.

It touched my heart to see how wonderful it was for people to help others less fortunate than themselves. What a marvelous way for us, the sound of body and mind, to exercise charity, one of the theological virtues—one of the surest of all stepping-stones to heaven and eternal happiness. It never occurred to me before that if all persons were self-sufficient, what outlet could love have? I was beginning to see the light, even the *good* in affliction.

The basis for my keener understanding came from a deeper, stronger faith. Faith was the key that opened the door and allowed the light to penetrate my beclouded thoughts. Unquestionably, love is the most important of all the virtues; it is the guiding force of all man's actions, but faith must come first as man cannot seek a goal if he does not believe in it.

All I have seen at St. Anne's has taught me to trust the Creator for all I have not seen. Saint Augustine explains this very clearly when he says, "Faith is to believe on the word of God what we do not see, and its reward is to see and enjoy what we believe."

I know that God could have performed a miracle and cured my baby. This would not have been a problem for Him. But God did not want me to believe in Him by seeing. Did He not say to "doubting" Thomas, "You became a believer because you saw me. Blest are they who have not seen and have believed" (Jn. 20:29)?

As I look around, there is evidence of God's presence and power everywhere. Every blade of grass, every tree that grows, every beautiful flower that blooms, and every baby that is born with its wonderful structure—all are miracles of divine wisdom and power. O my dear God, how could I ever doubt you!

Useful Purpose

It is so easy for me now to say that faith should not be difficult to acquire. But, really, if we only stop to think, faith is part of our daily life. Every day there are constantly happening

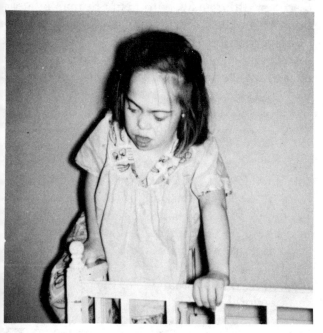

many things we do not understand that involve faith. In fact, many of us do not even think about them, but rather accept them without any doubt or question. For example, as we look into the sky on a clear night, the millions of twinkling stars challenge our imagination, especially when science tells us there are many millions more beyond our visual capacity to observe. The vastness of space staggers us. One might inquire, "Where does space begin, and does it have any end?" Although our brilliant scientists have discovered the answers to many of man's questions about the universe, the mysteries of creation are limitless. Happily, this does not unduly disturb us. Our faith in God assures us that everything He created has a good and useful purpose, thus every planet, even to the smallest star, has a reason for being where it is, if for no other *known* reason than to give glory to God.

So it is with my little Mary Margaret. She may be in her own little orbit, far removed from the intellects of society, but like the tiniest of stars in the heavens, millions of miles from nowhere, she, too, is a creation of the Master, and like all His other creations, she also has a good and useful purpose for being here.

I can only speculate why Mary Margaret was created. I do know that one of the greatest needs of this world is love, the basis for all peace and happiness. From the very beginning she seemed to be a symbol of love. I believe one good reason

Sunshine with Annette Schardt, who also has Down's Syndrome

God sent us this baby has been to show us the meaning of love, a love that acts, a love that sacrifices, a love that seeks union.

Sacred Scripture, over and over, brings us messages of love.

"This is the first [commandment]:
'...You shall love the Lord your God
   with all your heart,
   with all your soul,
   with all your mind,
   and with all your strength.'

This is the second,

'You shall love your neighbor as yourself.'
There is no other commandment greater than these" (Mk. 12:29-31).

You have already read that Mary Margaret possesses a dynamic, lovable personality. She has been mentioned as a little ray of sunshine who can change the whole gloomy world into a land of sunshine by just turning on her smile. Therefore, her purpose in this life is not only to awaken us spiritually, but also to add pleasure and joy to our lives. We must remember that "Sunshine" and all the handicapped help the strong become more charitable, more patient, and more Christian.

Some people thank God for little girls, others for little boys. We should thank God for all children, especially for the retarded. Yes, thank God for them; they teach us so much—they do such a great service.

This statement may bewilder you. Surely, I am not saying that mental retardation is something to be prized, and I do not propose that expectant parents pray for defective offspring! Certainly not. This would, indeed, be perverse. But it is not a matter of preference. In itself, mental retardation is a deficiency, an affliction. We should do everything possible to prevent and alleviate it, but if it should befall you, do not consider it a curse. Make the best of it by accepting it and putting it to work for you. It is one of the burdens that God permits, from which good, much good, can come. And it is in this sense that I can say, "Thank God for our retarded children."

Gratitude is a sentiment which can be evoked in various ways. This reveals another service which the retarded bring to us. When you see a retarded child, you have reason to count your blessings and be grateful that God has not permitted you or your children to be so under-privileged. If the retarded expands our hearts a little, if he helps us to be a little more grateful, if he brings us a little closer to God by pointing out His goodness, then the little child has fulfilled another purpose.

Recognizing True Values

It is so easy to understand how I failed to appreciate earlier the spiritual values of my

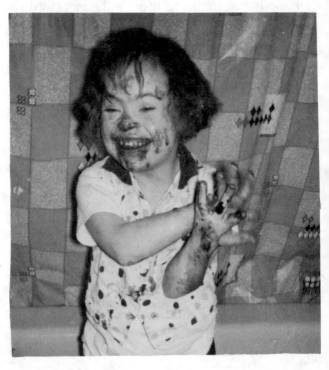

child, since even material values, the solid objects I can evaluate with my own physical faculties, are often misappraised by me.

Often, material products are practically worthless at the time of discovery, but as time moves on and conditions change, the values frequently soar to unpredictable heights. In the year 1626, Pete Minuit purchased a large tract of land, then known as New Amsterdam, from the Indians for only sixty guilders, approximately twenty-four dollars. Today, this same tract of land is known as Manhattan Island, New York.

Oil at one time, and not too long ago, had no value. In 1828, the Old American Well was drilled in the bed of Little Renox Creek, near Burkesville, Kentucky. The men were drilling for salt water, which was to be used for preserving food. Instead of the expected brine, the then worthless oil spurted twenty-five to thirty feet into the air and was allowed to flow wastefully downstream. The drillers were disappointed and considered themselves failures.

The largest diamond ever mined was the Cullinan. It weighed 3,106 carats before being cut. It was cut into 105 gems, the largest weighing 530.2 carats. The value of this *one* stone alone, in 1947, was $2,500,000. It is understandable why the cutting of the diamond, which gives value to the stone, is entrusted only to experts.

These are only a few examples where the practically worthless took on phenomenal value

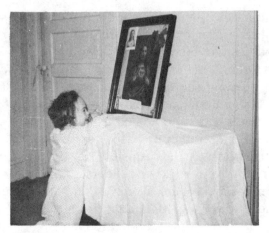

Sunshine saying her prayers

after conditions were changed, either by "Father Time" or by processing.

Is my cross of any value to me now? From a materialistic viewpoint, I cannot truthfully say yes. But, like the raw diamond, it is being processed by an Expert, and also like "New Amsterdam" and the "Old American Oil Well," which matured into inconceivable monetary value, time will most certainly prove the spiritual treasure it represents. When this day arrives for me, then a thousand present-day Manhattan Islands, plus all the flowing oil wells, and all the cut diamonds in all the world, if I owned them, would be of no value to me. The only things of any value to me will be those I take with me—the treasures stored in heaven.

When I think of eternity I realize how foolish we are when we don't consider it more seriously and make some definite plans towards our salvation. Eternity is part of our future, whether we want to think about it or not. No one ever escaped it by ignoring it. Ironically, we are an ambitious people who are always planning for the future. We sacrifice, struggle, toil, and even die to fulfill our dreams of a better tomorrow. All of this is good, displaying the results of an educated society, of which we are proud and which we wouldn't want any other way.

Yet, are we guilty of foolishly placing all our efforts into only temporary values? In all ages, gold has been the potential curse of mankind. To gain it men have yielded honor, affection, and lasting renown, and because of it bartered their crown to eternity. Placing too much emphasis on material values in this life recalls the story of the Gospel—"There was a rich man who had a good harvest. 'What shall I do?' he asked himself. 'I have no place to store my harvest. I know!' he said. 'I will pull down my grain bins and build larger ones. All my grain and my goods will go there. Then I will say to myself: You have blessings in reserve for years to come. Relax! Eat heartily, drink well. Enjoy yourself.' But God said to him, 'You fool! This very night your life shall be required of you. To whom will all this piled-up wealth of yours go?' That is the way it works with the man who grows rich for himself instead of growing rich in the sight of God" (Lk. 12:16-21).

After I arrived home from my second visit to St. Anne's, the thought of having a normal child, which had been so important to me before the trip to Beaupre, had little or no significance for me now. St. Anne, the expert with the afflicted, to whom I entrusted my troubles, went to work on my behalf, and, like the diamond cutter, polished and cut until, through her intercession, she gained for me the faith to see my cross not as a worthless waste, but as a valuable spiritual gem. She awakened me to the realization that we are created not only with a body, but also with an immortal soul, which also requires nourishment. Oh, my dear God, how often we are guilty of over-nourishing our bodies, but starving our souls!

Through St. Anne's guidance and loving care, I received the grace to see, understand, and accept God's holy will. When this was accomplished, a profound sense of peace came over me; I no longer was tortured with the ugly thoughts of being a Jekyll and Hyde, or a shiny car without a motor. For this favor I feel that I owe God a heavy debt of gratitude, one which is not in my power to ever repay. I am now most grateful to Him for permitting me to be the father of one of His special children. I am so pleased to be one of His privileged ones that I hope He might come and dwell in my happy and thankful heart.

As I look back, it seems incredible how I felt a few years ago. I feel ashamed even to think about it. But now my only regret is that my "Sunshine" is not twins. This is the way God answered my prayers. It may have taken me a long time to understand, but now I realize that God was answering my prayers from the very beginning, only I was not looking for spiritual values; I was asking for a miracle. But the way God answered my prayers is so much better than the physical miracle I pleaded for, and I was so unaware of it.

Describing "Sunshine"

To try to describe "Sunshine" other than I have already done is most difficult, as each person sees in her something uniquely precious. But perhaps this will explain her appeal just a little.

You, no doubt, have often watched a little girl play with her beautiful, favorite baby doll. It could be the one that Santa left under the Christmas tree, or the one perhaps she received for her third birthday. If you observe her closely, you become aware that she loves this little doll very much. She calls the doll by a very pretty name and makes playing "Mommy and baby" so real. The doll is handled with affectionate, tender care. It is rocked to sleep with a lullaby. The baby doll actually closes its eyes. It can cry and even shed tears. It talks and walks, moves its arms and legs, and can be made to stand on its head. It is bathed and given permanent waves, and can do almost everything Mommy's real, live baby can do. No wonder little girls are so proud of their very own baby dolls. Every time I watched one of these little mothers, I

believed that in their "make-believe world" they often made a wish that their pretty baby dolls might come to life just as Pinocchio became a real, live boy.

My "Sunshine" reminds me of just such a beautiful play baby doll, who has suddenly started to breathe. She walks, talks, closes her eyes, cries, claps hands, and oh so many other cute little things that a baby doll can't do. But with each motion she looks so much like a beautiful doll that sometimes I am almost tempted to look for the key that winds her up.

She has two beautiful blue eyes full of tender light, a dimple so sweet, two tiny hands, and two rosy feet. Her soul is as pure and white as the snow, and as long as she lives it will never be brushed with the slightest taint of sin. Her smile is adorable, and her laugh tinkles with joy. She is God's special gift to us—a precious bundle of joy.

Third Family Pilgrimage —Thanksgiving

It was early August 1959 when we made our third consecutive family pilgrimage to Saint Anne de Beaupre. "Sunshine" was now three years old, and although her little body had grown stronger, her accomplishments were still very slow, and we sincerely doubted if she ever would be strong enough to walk.

This year, however, instead of praying for a miracle, it was my intention to just have a good heart-to-heart talk with St. Anne and to thank God for giving me the grace to accept His holy will. As I stood beneath the miraculous statue of St. Anne, I moved my lips in silent prayer, which came from the depths of my thankful heart:

"Good St. Anne, I love my baby with all my heart. No greater love has any parent for his child than I have for Mary Margaret. In spite of this great love and affection I have for "Sunshine," will not my heart be tortured when people, through their ignorance, innocently make fun of her incapabilities? When such sad occasions do strike, dearest good St. Anne, please give me the strength to soothe my emotions, and help me recall the words of Jesus as He hung dying on the cross: "Father, forgive them; they do not know what they are doing" (Lk. 23:34).

"Also, St. Anne, did not your own daughter, Mary, the Mother of God, suffer seven terrible sorrows? Therefore, any sadness Alice and I might endure will be negligible in comparison to what your Virgin Daughter suffered. Please don't let me ever forget this.

"However, as a father, I am subject to human weaknesses. At times I may be tempted to ask everybody in heaven to intercede before the throne of God, asking Him to make my daughter normal in mind and in body. But please, St. Anne, overlook these pleas, as they will only be made in a moment of weakness, as I love "Sunshine" the way she is. Furthermore, I am grateful for everything He has given me. Thank Him for giving me such worthy, loving parents and relatives. Also, ask Him to please forgive all the numerous sins I have committed against Him. Ask Him also to give me the grace, the light, or whatever I need, to know Him better, for if I get to know Him better I will love Him more, and if I love Him more it will not be so easy for me to offend Him. Then ask Him please to help me to be a good father to the children He has so generously entrusted to my care.

"St. Anne, you have been a wonderful heavenly Grandmother to me. If I should ever forget you, please don't you forget me. I need you every day of my life."

As we left the Basilica for the third time, Alice told me that she made a promise to Saint Anne that we would return to the shrine again on another pilgrimage of thanksgiving if our Mary Margaret ever walked.

Spiritual Effects

What spiritual effects our little "Sunshine" will have on me, my family, relatives, and my friends, cannot be foreseen, and therefore cannot be written at this time. However, eventually we will all shed our clay shells and pass into a life of eternity in the next world. This story of Mary

At the home of dear friends, Mr. and Mrs. C. B. Lanman

Margaret, "Sunshine," will then be finished. At that time we might see her at the throne of God, surrounded by angels, sitting on the knee of her heavenly Father. He could be saying to her as we see Him extend His hand over a large multitude of people, "Well done, my little 'Sunshine.' All these people standing before me, because of you, received my message of love, faith, hope, and charity. You were the way and the light that led them to eternal happiness in my heavenly home." He then kisses her on the cheek and

Sunshine with her brother Bernie

says, "You may jump off my knee and enjoy for all eternity the wonders of heaven," which Saint Paul tried in vain to describe to the whole world: "You will now *see* and *hear,* and it will enter *into your heart,* all the marvelous things I have prepared for those who love me."

The Cross Is Not Heavy

Just a moment, please—I guess Mary Margaret is tired. She had a very busy day today. May 29, 1960, was her fourth birthday. She seemed to enjoy the extra-special attention we

made over her today. We had paper hats, horns, and the traditional cake and ice cream. The entire family had a merry time, and the baby especially enjoyed it when we all sang, "Happy Birthday, Sunshine." We helped her cut the cake and blow out the candles, but we didn't mind, as we are only too eager to help her, now and for all the years to come. Yes, the busy day wore her out, and now she is looking up at me with her little arms outstretched, and her beautiful clear, light blue eyes seem to say, "Please take me into your arms, Daddy." As I cuddle her close, she gives me the sweetest smile as if to say, "Thank you, Daddy," then she dozes off to sleep. She is still smiling as I carry her off to bed. It is so difficult now for me to believe that I at one time considered this precious bundle of joy and love *a cross*. Thank you, God, for performing a slow miracle, by turning my bitter cross into a symbol of love. If "Sunshine" is my cross, then it is no effort to take up my cross and follow you—I love my cross!

Epilogue

Four years have passed since *Slow Miracle* was written. Mary Margaret is now eight years old. Yes, in case you are wondering, she can walk now; she took her first steps in August 1960. We also kept our promise to St. Anne and made our fourth family pilgrimage to her shrine at Beaupre in thanksgiving.

"Sunshine" can say a few words, but cannot speak fluently. This does not handicap her too much, however, as she usually has ways of expressing her needs, and we usually have no trouble interpreting them.

My love for Mary Margaret has grown greater with the passing of each day. I feel it is useless to try to explain my feelings as people for the most part cannot understand. To me my retarded daughter is like finding a beautiful flower in a torrid, desolate desert. It becomes too precious to describe to just anyone, because not all can see the beauty in the flower as I do. So it is with my "Sunshine." My friends may smile and nod an expression of understanding for the gracious way

I now accept this child and love her, but somehow I sense their sentiments are more in the nature of sympathy. For no one can ever know or appreciate the affection and love I have for her, unless, of course, it is the baby's mother, her sister and brothers, the parents of other handicapped children, or possibly people who work with retarded children.

Regretfully, I have met a few people whose materialistic thinking and lack of faith in God have prompted them to insist that the retarded child is a reject of nature, a waste, and never will be of any value to society. They view the care and treatment of the retarded child with cold and impersonal logic. However, fortunately these people are few, and their concept of the retarded person is as outdated as the horse and buggy in this day of speedy methods of transportation.

During the past eight years I have found that the majority of people have awakened to the fact that the mentally retarded, like the blind, the crippled, and all the other handicapped, have God-given rights based on the dignity of their human personality endowed with an immortal soul. This right entitles all the handicapped to be considered eligible for the best treatment that society can give them as human beings.

In keeping with this thought and realizing that something must be done to train the mentally retarded child, an organization was founded in our community, "The Trumbull County Council for Mentally Retarded Children." This hard-working group created a Speakers Bureau and other forms of information to acquaint the

public with problems of mental retardation
—what is being done to help—and to win "acceptance" for the retarded child. The general public
responded most generously, understandingly,
and many were stunned at the lack of provision
for the retarded child. With the public's support,
the Council accomplished much towards helping
these children to live more useful and happy
lives.

One of the greatest achievements of the
Council was to present the voters of Trumbull
County a tax levy to provide a school for mentally retarded school-age children. This levy
passed in 1961, which resulted in a beautiful,
modern ten-room building named, "Fairhaven."
This was the first tax-supported school in Trumbull County, Ohio, for the mentally retarded.

Fairhaven School gave to the parents of the
retarded child a new hope and a sense of pride in
realizing that their child was no longer a reject,
but was accepted in a tax-supported school just
like other children in their schools. The entire
community also took pride in the fact that they,
the people, by voting for the school levy, made it
possible for these long neglected, forgotten
children to at last receive the training and
discipline of which they were so long deprived.

The retarded child is no longer relegated to a
useless and passive life. In special schools where
"Sunshine" is able to play with other handicapped children, she is constantly stimulated

Sunshine's class at Fairhaven

and has learned things she never could learn at home. "Sunshine" is very happy and well adjusted in the classroom, and I am thankful to all those wonderful people who made it possible for her to have the opportunity to go to school and develop her efficiency to the highest level of her mental limitation.

Yes, today the mentally handicapped are fortunate in having many earthly friends, but we should take note also of their spiritual benefactors—their "heavenly friends."

We have the word of God for the fact that the angels have befriended "these little ones." "I assure you, their angels in heaven constantly behold my heavenly Father's face" (Mt. 18:10). If every child of God is cherished by a guardian angel, how the angels of the retarded must love them!

And no words can better verify the best of all the friends of the retarded than those which Jesus Christ Himself uttered in a rebuke and yet so lovingly. " 'Let the children come to me and do not hinder them. It is to just such as these that the kingdom of God belongs....' Then he embraced them and blessed them, placing his hands on them" (Mk. 10:14, 16). The retarded always remain as little children.

There is no need for me to worry about the future years for "Sunshine." "Look at the birds in the sky. They do not sow or reap, they gather nothing into barns; yet your heavenly Father feeds them. Are not you more important than they?" (Mt. 6:26) Therefore, I believe that heaven will watch over "Sunshine" all the days of her life. How could it be any other way?

"Sunshine" will never be a brilliant student, a loving mother, or a successful career woman. A few short years ago these thoughts frightened me almost to a point of despair. How foolish it was of me to place so much value on dreams that may never have come true anyhow, even if she had been born with a healthy, normal body and mind. For who of us can say for certain what tomorrow will bring? My Faith has given me confidence that "Sunshine" is assured a place in heaven, which is all that really matters. Saint

Augustine once said of success: "The only unsuccessful person on earth is the unfortunate person who ends up in hell for all eternity." Therefore, "Sunshine" is a success; she *will* reach the goal (heaven) which is really the primary purpose for man's creation—God made us to know Him, to love Him, to serve Him in this world and to be happy with Him forever in the next.

"Let Us Not Forget"

Do not look forward to the trials and crosses of life with fear. God, to whom you belong, will deliver you from them as they arise. God has guided you and guarded you until now. Hold fast to His strong hand, and He will lead you safely

through all trials. The same good Father who cares for you today will take good care of you tomorrow and on every day of your life. Either He will shield you from suffering or He will give you the unfailing strength to bear it. Be at peace and rest in the arms of your heavenly Father and thank God always for every gift He has given you.

In Conclusion

When I had finished writing this little story I knelt down with the manuscript in my folded hands, and with bowed head I prayed:

"My dear God, I believe from the bottom of my heart that this story is the message I received through my daughter, Mary Margaret. This message had such a profound effect upon me, I want

to share it with others. For this reason, I have tried to become an assistant to 'Sunshine,' to help her deliver Your message to my friends and neighbors. This is my first attempt at writing a story, and believe me, I found it difficult to put into words the feelings that were locked in my heart. Whether or not I have been successful I do not know, but I did try—I did my best. It was required of me that I reveal my innermost feelings, which by nature would have remained tightly sealed within my heart. But if what I have written helps just one person to know You a little better and to love You a little more, and if it makes someone's cross a little lighter, then all my efforts will be more than richly rewarded. Thanks, my dear God, for everything.''

PART TWO

Messenger of God's Love

Our Gift of Love

Sixteen years have sped by since the story of our "Sunshine" was written. We have been gratified by the tremendous interest and sharing of heartfelt experiences it has evoked. Your out-

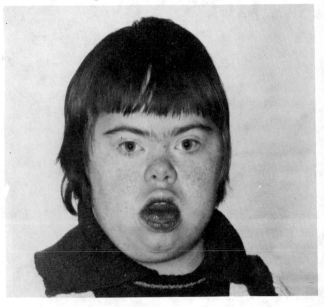

pouring of love in your letters has enriched the lives of myself and my family. Many of you have been asking—"How is 'Sunshine' today?" "Is your personal regard for her still the same?" "Is your appreciation of her value the same as it was thirteen years ago?"

Let me answer the last question first, since I am sure you will agree it is the most important.

Yes, my love for her and appreciation of her value to me *and to others* have been, like the mighty oak, growing more beautiful, richer, and more encompassing. Through the years, they have been watered and fed by the grace of her presence and love.

More than ever, I am convinced today that this child of God has a special mission that is hers alone, a message of love. We know that God works through His people to manifest His love and power. As mysterious as it may seem, He chose this retarded child with an I.Q. of only thirty to awaken hearts and minds to His great love, but first and foremost—my own heart! The weak He has chosen to open the unseeing eyes of those thought to be wise.

"SUNSHINE'S" BIRTHDAY

Memorial Day—May 29, 1978. Today is Mary Margaret's ("Sunshine's") birthday. There is no better time to begin to update a story than

on the anniversary of the "celebrity." It hardly seems possible that twenty-two years have gone by since Dr. Allan Altdoerffer broke the shocking news to me that our new baby girl was mongoloid.

It is the custom in our family, regardless of whose birthday it is, young or old, to celebrate the occasion with cake and ice cream. We all look forward to birthday parties, because they have for us a very special meaning. To us, they mean the opportunity to show the very special love and respect we have for one another. Not only that, our hearts are filled with gratitude to the Creator for bringing us together, one by one, to form a wonderful, united, loving and happy family. I am very proud to be their father; I know of no person richer than I—my family is my incalculable wealth.

Today, it's "Sunshine's" turn to be honored. All of us are gathered around the dining room table ready for her mother to bring in the beautifully decorated cake she baked earlier in the day. The dining room lights are turned off, and she appears in the doorway holding the cake with twenty-two flickering candles, and everyone is singing, "Happy birthday, 'Sunshine.'" "Sunshine's" eyes flicker brighter than the candles, because she loves parties and this one is all for her. Her hands are clapping and her arms are waving in gestures of delight. There is a small hurricane of laughter and delight as we all help her to blow out the candles, and her mother's hand carefully guides as "Sunshine" cuts her cake. Though she cannot express herself in words, she is well aware of what is taking place.

The blowing out of the candles is not easy for "Sunshine," even though it can be amusing. With her lips closed, she will build up a pressure of air that will make her little cheeks look like half baseballs. Then stretching her head as close to the burning candles as she dares, she will blow as hard as she can. But despite her great effort, she cannot extinguish the forest of flaming wax by herself. So, one of us always gives her an unknown assistance. The curling smoke that

remains fascinates her, and she makes a great effort at singing, "Happy Birthday," but since the words are too difficult for her, she hums the tune which she knows very well. She can hum the melodies of several when her mood is right, and she does a good job.

After the ice cream and cake, "Sunshine" is ready for her birthday gifts of love and admiration from us all. She has no knowledge whatsoever of material values. It just doesn't seem to matter whether the gift be big, small, expensive or inexpensive. She shows equal appreciation for each beautifully wrapped package. She needs a little help to open them but, of course, we are careful that she is the one to unravel that last bit of ribbon, that last piece of paper, and reveal the contents for herself. For all of us at the birthday party, this is the high point. As "Sunshine" sees the gift, holding it in her hand, we are treated to her very own unique expression of gratitude. She will tilt her head to one side, pucker her lips as if to whistle, squint her oriental eyes and wave her little arms like the slow flapping wings of a bird. It is really hard to describe. You must see her facial and body movements, these strong expressions of pleasure and gratitude. It is a treat that warms the heart.

It takes "Sunshine" to make birthdays really glow with love.

"SUNSHINE"—EVERY DAY

Every day is a little life; and our whole life is but a day—repeated.

"Sunshine's" days are all just about the same—"very daily"—very routine. The ten hours she sleeps every night should be more than sufficient to wind her up with renewed energy. But, just like her daddy, when it is time to crawl out of a comfortable bed, with a disarming look, she pleads for that extra few minutes we would

all like to capture—just this once. Of course, the daily schedule harbors no place for time-consuming sleepy wishes; so "Sunshine" rises and shines with the rest of the family, even though at this early hour she is on "low glow" with the rest of us.

And then there is her mom, Alice. She should wear a sign: "Maternal Love—Never Off Duty." And she does, the sign of love. It's there, not only in what she does for all the rest of us, but in the unending care and watchfulness of her very special child. She is the gentle hand of love that turns "Sunshine" on full glow, bathing, dressing, serving her breakfast as the kitchen clock ticks off the moments till the Fairhaven school bus opens its door to pick her up and deliver her on time to school. Alice is her guardian angel all day, every day, and it's been that way since God first sent "Sunshine" to us.

Every morning I like to play a little game with "Sunshine." Usually she has a good start eating her breakfast by the time I arrive downstairs. From the angle where I enter the dinette, her back is always towards the door which makes it easy for me to play my game. I will tip-toe across the small room and very slowly and gently cover her two eyes with my hands. Then I will say to her, "Guess who it is," and she will promptly reply, "Paa." I will then make a fuss, making it known to her that she guessed correctly. I will give her a prize by bending down and kissing her on the cheek which she seems to enjoy. Her brothers, particularly Jimmy, thinks this is really something, and he will try the same procedure. But even though his voice doesn't sound like mine, he gets a very disappointing reply. Instead of "Sunshine" saying, "Jimmy," she will respond with, "Paa." But Jim wants her to say his name so badly he will keep telling her over and over again, "No, not Paa, say 'Jimmy.' " When he repeats this often enough, eventually she will get it right and please her brother by saying, "Gemmee." To this, Jim will feel very proud; his endurance or patience paid off. But, the very next day when he tries the same routine, "Sunshine" forgets all about Jimmy's coaching and will again respond with "Paa." This performance gives a good laugh to everyone who sees it. Just another asset we chalk up to "Sunshine," because a good-natured laugh is worth a hundred groans in any market.

Alice, with "Sunshine" in hand and our dog Peppie along as a faithful sentinel, leaves the house a little early as it is a slow procedure for "Sunshine" to walk down the steps to the sidewalk. "Sunshine" is not very active and so she needs all the exercise she can get. With this in mind, rather than just standing on the sidewalk, waiting for the bus, Alice will make a little game of walking slowly back and forth with her until the yellow bus makes its way up the street.

At 7:45 A.M., as Alice helps "Sunshine" on the bus, the other children greet her with, "Hello, Mrs. Sunshine,"—"Hi, Mrs. Sunshine." Innocence, love and warmth abound in the greetings of these children. This warms Alice's heart.

The bus driver, Mrs. Ruth Miranda, has a very evident compassion for all of these passengers on the little yellow mini-bus; one of them is her own child, Tommy. They are on their way by 7:50 A.M., bye-byeing and waving, with the nose of many a smiling face pressed against the window glass.

After being in school for seven hours, "Sunshine" is happy to get home again. Alice and "Sunshine" stand on the corner as the bus pulls away amid happy cries of, "Goodbye, 'Sunshine' "—"Goodbye, Mrs. Sunshine," and much arm waving.

Once home, "Sunshine" changes into her playclothes and then will either play records or thumb through a magazine until it is time for supper.

Children with Down's Syndrome are known to be lovers of music, perhaps because they are so close to the angels. Poets tell us music is the speech of the angels. "Sunshine" loves it. She has her own record player, a hand model, not

automatic. It plays just one record at a time. And
she manipulates it as well as any disc jockey,
turning it on and off and changing the records
and making any necessary adjustments. There is
just one way she likes to listen to records and
that is *loud,* with the volume turned all the way
up. Thomas Edison has furnished her with many
hours of entertainment. We have found no
substitute. Nothing even comes close to making
''Sunshine's'' recreational time this happy. If

Mr. Edison were still around today, I would make a point of thanking him personally; as it is, he's remembered in my prayers.

Second to the record player are magazines and catalogs. She likes to look at the pictures and associate them with her everyday surroundings. When time permits, we will scan through the book with her. When a picture of a dog appears, she will point to it, and because she cannot pronounce the word "dog" clearly, she will say, "bow-wow." An automobile is a "kah"; a baby is a "bebbie." Some words she will make an attempt to say, others she won't even try.

She becomes so wrapped up in what she is doing that she never comes to the dinner table when we call her. One of us must approach her, pat her on the head and tell her that it is time to eat. She immediately puts down her magazine, shuts off the record player, hops off her chair, and scoots into the dining room.

About 6:30 or 7:00 in the evening, "Sunshine" is ready for bed. We don't have to tell her; she tells us by joining her two hands together, placing them against her cheek, closing her eyes and imitating a snore. When she is ready for bed, she is very insistent. After all, it is unusual for a child to want to go to bed so early. Either Alice or I oblige. It gives us a reprieve from the repeated loud noise of the record player. The house takes on a welcome strange quiet for another few hours.

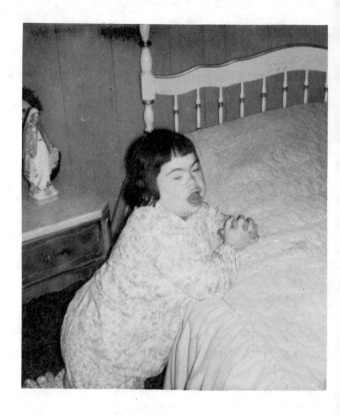

There is another lesson we have learned from the retarded. As anxious as "Sunshine" is to get to bed, she will not do so until she first kneels down to pray. From her earliest days, we taught "Sunshine" to talk to God. She may not have the intelligence to know the real value of prayer, but, I repeat, she will not get into bed until she first talks to God. Even as Abraham Lincoln has said, "I have been driven many times to my knees by the overwhelming conviction that I had nowhere else to go. My own wisdom and that of all about me seemed insufficient for the day.''

Of course, "Sunshine" cannot, by herself, pray. But, with folded hands and her eyes looking at the crucifix on the wall, she very devoutly listens to Alice or me ask God for His blessings upon our family and friends, to bring peace into the world and turn hardened hearts to love. We thank Him for all the good things He has given us, and we close by asking Him to make "Sunshine" an instrument of His love to bring people closer to Him and the love He is so willing to share. After a Sign of the Cross and a "Goodnight to God," "Sunshine" jumps into bed. Alice or I tuck the covers around her, and we are instantly rewarded with a heavenly hug or kiss. If during the day we made any sacrifices; if the music from the record player was extra loud; if she caused any extra work; if she caused any inconvenience—that hug, that kiss makes it worth it. As we close her bedroom door, silently we thank God for entrusting us with her care.

A FEW OF "SUNSHINE'S" FAVORITES

One of "Sunshine's" favorites is music. Jazz, rock, nursery rhymes, folk, country western,

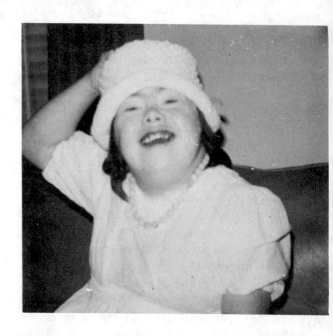

you name it; but her favorite is polka. "Sunshine" loves a fast beat. Many times when such a record is playing, she will get off her chair and start to dance by herself, swinging her arms and body just like the other kids do. She has dancing at school too. Thomas Alva Edison should be blessed twice.

Pretty, colorful clothes are high on her list of priorities. She loves to be all dressed-up. Strange as it may seem, she seems to know the time and place for wearing her dress-up clothes. When the occasion is over, like after church on Sunday, she will insist on changing into her more comfortable playclothes.

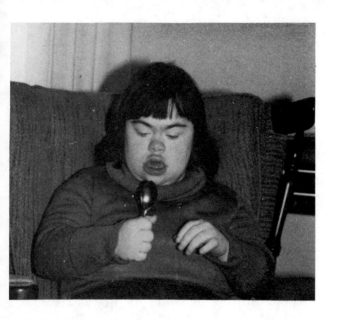

It is difficult to find the right fit for her in the stores, and this again is where Alice's magic saves the day. Her talents as a seamstress with needle and thread express themselves in the creations she makes for "Sunshine" and the warmth that once again her devotion and love pass on to us all.

"Sunshine's" favorite toy, above and beyond all others, is the common teaspoon. She calls it a "poon." In your travels, if you ever come across a sweet little girl, four feet, two inches tall, weighing 115 pounds, brown hair with bangs, round face with slanty, blue eyes, holding a teaspoon in her short stubby fingers, you have met "Sunshine." She loves to hold a spoon and not just any spoon. It has to be a particular one, plain, lightweight and dull. When she first decided that this was her favorite toy, we had a few of them around the house, but now we are down to the very last one. Needless to say, we try our very best to guard this spoon like the government watches over the gold in the vaults at Fort Knox. This is understandable because there is no substitute for this special spoon. Often we tried to pawn off other "poons" but she would only look at another "poon," study it, and refuse to accept it. This really creates a problem. For when she misplaces it, and this happens quite frequently, everybody in the house joins in the search with the thought "nothing is lost that a thorough search will not find it." Also, we keep St. Anthony, patron saint of lost articles, busy with our petitions for his help. We search under the couch, behind chairs, upstairs, downstairs. In other words, we just about turn the house inside out. There are times when we just have to give up. Then, luckily, the spoon will turn up in the most unexpected place. But, there will come the day when our luck will run out and "Sunshine" will just have to adopt a new toy, at least until the time her spoon shows up.

Two years ago while vacationing in Gettysburg, Pennsylvania, I spied one of these favorite spoons in the "Battlefront Cafeteria" restaurant. I explained to the manager why I wanted to purchase this particular spoon. When

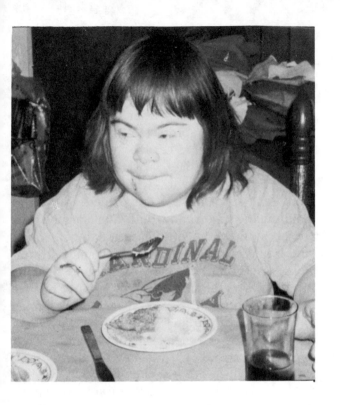

he heard my story, he gave me a couple of spoons for "Sunshine" with a smile and his blessing.

EATING HABITS

Shakespeare once said, "An enterprise, when fairly once begun, should not be left till all that ought is won."

I believe "Sunshine" was about five years old when we began to teach her to feed herself. This was an early time for her in spite of her age. I remember very vividly what a terrible mess she would make. We protected the floor with a washable covering, as her food would drop from the highchair tray. Her face and protective bib would be covered with whatever was on the menu. She also had a habit of getting tired of handling the spoon and would give it a good toss, aiming it nowhere, but occasionally it would land on my necktie. Washing food stains off our clothes, scrubbing the baby's chair and cleaning the floor were almost everyday affairs. But we thought that, in order to be successful, we must toil awhile, endure awhile, believe always, and never turn back. It took time, but eventually our perseverance paid off, and she gained very good eating habits. However, when we decided that she was ready to eat in a restaurant, we were a little concerned as to how she would act. With a prayer in our hearts and on our lips, we were brave enough to give it a try. Any fears that we might have had were unwarranted. She behaved very well in public eating places, just like any other young lady would. We were so happy that she had learned her lessons well, and we are so proud of her table manners, both at home and in public.

I remember the doctor telling us that these children like starchy foods above all others. This proved to be true with "Sunshine." Her favorites are spaghetti, macaroni, potatoes. However, we don't have these on the menu every night, and she usually enjoys eating whatever is on her plate. I came to the conclusion that eating is another one of her favorite pastimes. One surprising note: Usually children don't care for green beans. (At least this was our experience with our other children.) Well, "Sunshine" loves them; she will not leave one bean on her plate. She eats vegetables but not with the same zest as the green beans.

The doctor also warned us that overweight is common among mongoloid children. This is primarily attributed to lack of exercise and to eating the starchy foods they enjoy so much. "Sunshine's" overweight was a gradual process which totally escaped our attention until recently. We now are faced with a big problem in trying to control her food intake. She just doesn't understand why she can't have that second, third, or fourth serving of potatoes.

AWARENESS

There are times when "Sunshine" will amaze us with her awareness. We often say that we don't give her enough credit for what she knows, and because she cannot communicate like normal people, we often wonder just what

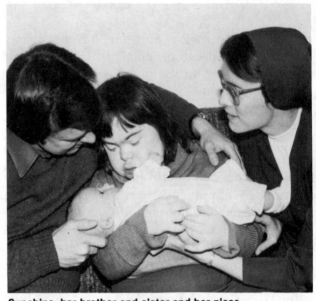

Sunshine, her brother and sister and her niece.

she is thinking about. For example: She loves other children, especially little ones or babies. Our granddaughter, Lynn Marie, three years old, lives about eight blocks from us. When we drive in that direction, even before we reach the street, "Sunshine" recognizes the familiar neighborhood and in her own way lets us know she wants to visit the "bebbie." And when we don't stop to visit, "Sunshine" shows her disappointment by pouting a little, just as a normal child would.

The following instance amazed us beyond words. I drove into McDonald's parking lot, turned off the motor, and went into the building to get our order of goodies. It was a busy time of day and the waiting line was long. I decided to do a little shopping and come back later. When I got back into the car, "Sunshine" noticed I did not have the usual bag of hamburgers, and as I was about to start the motor, quick as a flash, she reached and touched the ignition key. She knew quite well that turning the key had something to do with moving the car. She could not tell us in words, but in her own way again she let us know that she didn't want to leave this restaurant without her hamburger and milkshake.

It is unusual happenings like these that continue to amaze us. If a normal child acted in a similar manner, we would not give it a second thought, but with "Sunshine" we are always surprised when she is so observant.

MEETING THE PUBLIC

When weather and health permit, we take "Sunshine" to meet the public. From the very start, we were never ashamed, never hid or sheltered her from the eyes of others. I believe by this attitude we not only did ourselves a great justice, but also helped to make the public aware that these children, like the blind and crippled, belong to society and are not to be abandoned by it. I am certain the publicity given to "Sunshine"

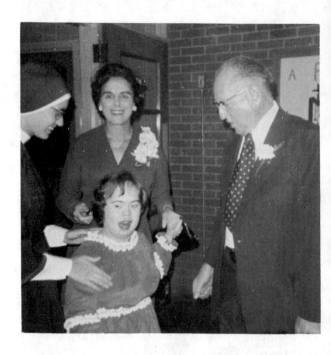

by the local newspapers was very instrumental in helping to get the initial tax levy passed in Trumbull County for the first tax-supported school for the retarded. In fact, a picture of "Sunshine" was used on a brochure that promoted the levy. This publicity made her well known throughout the area. It made Alice and I feel so good when strangers would recognize her on the street and stop to say a few cheery words to her.

Going to church was another excellent way for her to meet different people and learn to be in a crowded area. Each of our children, rain or shine, attended Mass every Sunday. "Sunshine" was no exception because of her retardation. On the contrary, getting "Sunshine" accustomed to attend church was good both for her and our fellow parishioners. She became aware of strangers mingling around her, and thus learned that there are others besides her immediate family. She also learned that she was in a house that was somehow very special and different. The parishioners, with their hearts full of sympathy, prayed for her and all the afflicted, and also in gratitude thanked God that they or their loved ones were spared this handicap.

It is good that we have reminders to thank God for all the blessings He gives us. To me, attending Sunday church services was always a serious obligation. You see, besides "Sunshine," who really put my faith to a good test, there was another wonderful lady in my life who taught me from the cradle the basics of my faith, which proved to be so useful throughout my life. This grand lady was my mother. Mom was never rich in material things, but her great faith in God and His Church more than compensated for this deficit. In spite of all her heartaches and adversities, she was a very happy woman. Since I am on the subject of going to church, I believe it is only fitting that I tell you a little about Mom, for it was she who drilled into me the real values of life—God, His Church, and His teachings.

As I look back over the years I understand now as I never understood before how much my mother loved me and my three brothers, Joe, Paul, and Otto. Her sacrifices must have been torturous, made bearable only by her great faith and love.

Today, I have friends, yes, fond, dear friends, but never will I have again the inexpressible love and gentleness lavished upon me by my mother. Only when I became a mature person did I fully realize all that Mom meant to me; then it was too late to let her know.

In 1918, when Dad died during the great flu epidemic, Mom was left practically penniless with four small children. In those days Social Security was unheard of; in fact, there was not much public help of any kind. Usually, in such circumstances it was the orphan home for the children. However, Mom was determined to keep the family together. She labored hard, taking in washing and ironing, scrubbing floors, and with a little help from loving relatives, somehow managed to keep the wolf away. God gave her just thirteen years of this life of sacrifice.

Mom never had much education, perhaps to the sixth or seventh grade, but she was our teacher in so many things. Her heart was her schoolroom, and learning and wisdom that could never be derived from a textbook flowed from it.

Mom was a great believer in the words that Jesus spoke, ''Give to Caesar the things that are Caesar's and to God the things that are God's.'' I also remember how she impressed upon us that we were created with two sides—a body and a soul. "We must go to school," she said, "to get a good education and prepare us for worldly goals, and to obtain a share of the better things of the world to have and enjoy. Likewise, the soul, just like the body, must be taken care of properly and nourished. Attending church, hearing and reading Holy Scriptures furnish us with these necessities." She warned us kids never to ignore the soul, for if the soul is ignored this creates problems—we get out of balance. If I never thanked you before, Mom, for your words of wisdom, I thank you now.

Alice also came from a family with similar religious background. When we were married thirty-seven years ago in our parish church of St. Canice, in Knoxville, Pittsburgh, Pennsylvania, we both saw our religion as a great bond and duty to God, lending true value to our existence. We were quite aware that God and His Church were alive in both of us as truly as we were alive in one another. Then when God blessed us with our priceless family, we saw to it that each child was not only aware, but also knowledgeable of God and His teachings. The precious heritage that we received from our parents we proudly passed on to our children. Like all parents who want the best for their children, we were no exception. We certainly wanted our children's future to be built on a firm foundation and not on sand. For Alice and me, it was always a beautiful

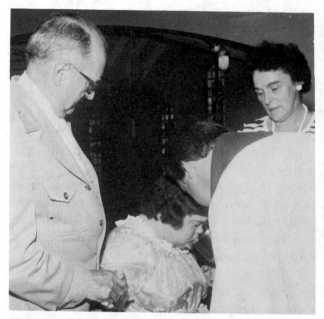

Sunshine receiving her first Holy Communion from the cup. Her brother Bernard is the priest—1979

and rewarding sight on Sunday morning when we glanced to our right or left and saw our children with their hands folded in prayer, talking to God the best way they knew how.

Usually we attend the nine-thirty Mass at St. Rose Church in Girard. Danny Martin, a good friend and a wonderful person, sits in the pew directly in front of us. For a couple of Sundays, as "Sunshine" was getting into her seat, she noticed Danny's neatly combed white hair, stopped, and gently kissed it. The kiss was so tender I doubt if it disturbed even one strand of his hair. Furthermore, Danny was so engrossed in his spiritual meditations, he was not aware of the affection extended to him. But from the smiles of approval from those who did witness this, especially Danny's gracious wife, Charlotte, they were all aware of this outward expression of love.

After the congregation recites the Lord's Prayer, the priest utters the words so often said by Jesus, "Peace be with you." The people turn to their neighbors standing next to them and greet one another with a sign of peace, usually a warm handshake. "Sunshine" loves this part of the Mass. She goes all out in extending her little hands to everyone around her, to the right, to the left, and to the folks in front of her. From the smiles and warmth on their faces, they are most anxious to share the sign of peace with "Sunshine." They know deep in their hearts this little girl is special. Usually after the excitement is over for her, "Sunshine" will again turn to me and look straight up into my eyes. Her little arms reach for me and her eyes have the sparkle of a couple of beautiful, large, perfect-cut, blue diamonds, and to me they seem to say, "I love you, Daddy. I want to kiss you"—my heart and mind yearn to embrace her. I do so with tender love and affection. When I free myself from her embrace, I wipe away my tears that so uncontrollably flow down my cheeks. There is a certain sacredness in these tears; they speak more eloquently than a thousand tongues. They are the messengers of overwhelming joy, and of unspeakable love. What a heavenly feeling at the Eucharist time of the Mass to hold a special child of God in my arms—a living saint. How thankful I am to be her father.

COMMUNICATIONS

The Chinese have a saying that an unlucky word dropped from the tongue cannot be brought back again by a coach drawn by six horses.

"Sunshine" will never be guilty of misusing her tongue. She will never injure another's character by idle gossip; I am especially sure of this since her vocabulary is very limited. Surpris-

ingly, she seems to understand every word of our English language, but can pronounce only a few words. Despite her mental handicap, she has formulated an effective means of communication. For example, when she wants to call our attention to our granddaughter, Lynn Marie, she will fold her arms and rock them back and forth and say "bebbie." To tell us that she wants her sunglasses from the glove compartment in the car, she will spread her thumb and index finger as wide as they will stretch and move her hand in this position toward our eyes. Occasionally, Alice will dress "Sunshine" in a short-sleeved blouse. If it is chilly, "Sunshine" will rub her arms and at the same time she will pretend to shiver and say "brrr." In other words, she wants to wear a sweater. Another one of her signs is to stretch her index finger and rub it against her lips to indicate that she wants to brush her teeth. There are many other signs, but these few I have mentioned to give you an idea of how she communicates her wants and desires to us.

All of these self-made gestures are very fascinating to us and we marvel at her ingenuity in devising these symbols entirely by herself. For the most part, without any trouble, we understand immediately. But there are times when we are perplexed. This puzzlement on our part has no adverse effect on us, but rather is a means for us to enjoy a good chuckle. This happens primarily at the dinner table. Perhaps she doesn't point

Coloring Easter eggs

straight, or our eyes don't see true, but
sometimes we have trouble guessing what "Sunshine" is "asking" for. (Aren't we blessed to
have many food items on our tables when very
many people in the world are going hungry?)
When we select the wrong items, she will shake
her head in a "no" motion. Sometimes she will
even say the word "no" very clearly. The guessing will continue until we hit on the item she
really wants. I surmise she gets a little impatient
with us when it takes us a while to understand
her wants, because when we guess the right
food, she nods her head "yes," claps her hands
and gives us that heavenly smile again.

OTHER THAN ROUTINE

"Sunshine" is a very good little traveler, much better than I. This could be due to her early exposure to lengthy rides when we took her to St. Anne's in Quebec, visiting relatives in Pittsburgh, and when her older sister entered the Community of the Daughters of Charity in Emmitsburg, Maryland. But regardless of the reason, the weariness or boredom from riding mile after mile for hours does not faze her at all. Like a good soldier, she never gives us any problems.

What "Sunshine" enjoys most when riding, however, is the car hitting a pothole in the road. When this happens, as you are aware, there is a thundering sound; "Sunshine" loves this noise and laughs delightedly. Naturally, we don't see anything funny about this; but she laughs so hard that we, too, find ourselves laughing and, forgetting about the possible damage to the car, look only to the brighter side.

In her innocence, "Sunshine" may at times create an embarrassing situation. One of these moments was generated when we decided to take advantage of J.C. Penney's portrait bargains. Everything was going very smoothly until the pretty young photographer stooped over to straighten a pleat in "Sunshine's" dress. I guess "Sunshine" did not like her pretty hairdo or the shade of blond hair. In any event, quicker than a wink, her little hand flashed out and grabbed the girl's hair which proved to be a wig. Fortunately, the pleasant and understanding young lady took this all very good-naturedly; she never lost her composure, almost as if it were a common occurrence and part of her job. I was amazed at how she laughed this off and considered it a big joke on herself. Thank God for people like her who can smile instead of frown; they are the truly happy ones. If more people would practice cheerfulness, they would accomplish more in less time, do it better, and persevere in it longer than the sad or grouchy person.

SOME PROBLEMS

The trials of life come to us not to make us sad, but sober; not to make us sorry, but wise; not to make us despondent, but by their darkness to refresh us as the night refreshes the day; not to impoverish, but to enrich us, as the plow enriches the field; and to multiply our joy, as the seed planted is multiplied a thousandfold.

Although we consider ourselves privileged that God has entrusted us to be the parents of one of His exceptional children, this does not mean that our daily lives are always a bed of sweet roses. No, there are many adjustments to be made, many considerations, many sacrifices. Patience and understanding are important qual-

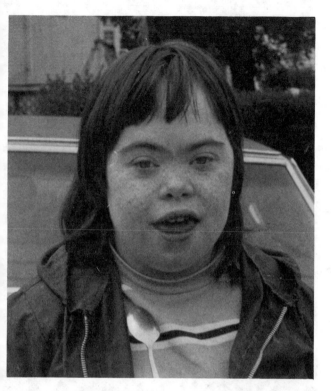

ities to possess. It is only to be expected that some problems will arise. "Sunshine" needs almost constant help. Help in getting bathed and dressed, help in putting on her boots in nasty weather. Due to her weak arches, she has difficulty walking; she cannot walk fast or for long distances. Trying to go down steps, and getting in and out of the car are usually chores and take time. These are only a few of the problems. I know there are many more, but why try to count them when we consider them all as minor.

However, in the midst of all these inconveniences, because we have faith in God, all our trials become as small ripples on the surface of the sea. Then again, we must consider that even normal, healthy children require many sacrifices from their loving parents. In many cases, they bring to their parents even torturous heartaches —much greater than the ones we endure with "Sunshine."

We are forever thankful that "Sunshine" does not give us any big worries or serious moral or civil problems. She is a most loving child and

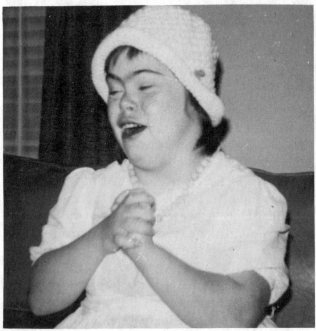

fits right in with the entire family. She is truly one of us, and every member of the family agrees that we would be missing a very precious jewel if she were not here with us. I often recall the sympathetic words of Doctor Allen Altdoerffer, "The mongoloid child is compatible, lovable and never known to become dangerous. For this alone, you should be thankful. The only real difference in a mongoloid child is his slow physical development and ability to learn. He must be made to feel that he is loved and wanted as a member of the family." I also remember another piece of cherished advice that he gave us. "If you have love in your hearts for this child, you will find room in your home."

HEALTH

"Sunshine" has outgrown the upper respiratory ailment that plagued her earlier years, and threatened to claim her young life.

However, one fall she developed a lump in her abdomen. Our family physician, Doctor Louis Zeller, suggested that we make an appointment with our surgeon. You might suspect that this caused us unreasonable concern. Actually, we had no right to fear and we should not have let this happen to us. After the initial shock of suspecting the worst, we placed our full faith in God and placed our anxiety to rest. Dr. Alexander Phillips examined "Sunshine" very thoroughly and assured us that she had a small hernia that could be repaired without any danger. Believe me when I say that we breathed a sigh of relief when we heard this diagnosis. The operation was a complete success, and we were again amazed that her stay in St. Elizabeth's Hospital was only three days, and her recovery at home was uneventful.

"Sunshine's" arches are very weak and this condition makes it necessary for her to wear special shoes fitted with orthopedic arch supports. If we are successful in reducing her food intake, this will no doubt benefit her arches.

Mongoloids are noted to have poor coordination, and "Sunshine" is no exception. In her case, I am not positive if the problem is due entirely to poor coordination, excessive weight, or arches, or a combination of all three. In any event, these physical problems tend to impede her ability to engage in active, healthful exercises which are so essential for the maintenance of good, sound health. However, everything being considered, "Sunshine" is strong and is enjoying good health.

"Sunshine's" physical and mental status does not necessarily apply to all who have Down's Syndrome. Without professional statistics, and using only my personal powers of observation, I find that mongoloids vary both in degrees of intelligence and of physical activities.

Mrs. Irene Hazel and Ronnie—1980

For example, I have seen some, although somewhat awkward in their efforts, get along very nicely riding two-wheeled bicycles, roller-skating, swimming, playing various games such as bowling, basketball and volleyball.

To make my observation clearer or more understandable, I will tell you about Ronnie Hazel who also has Down's Syndrome. I have already mentioned that "Sunshine's" I.Q. is very low. On the other hand, at the age of seven, Ronnie had an I.Q. that was too high to attend the Mahoning County School for the Retarded. Therefore, it was necessary for Ronnie to attend a special education class at Sheridan School for two years before the educators finally decided that the Retarded School was best for him.

Ronnie is now sixteen years old; he has two brothers, Father Terry (a Catholic priest) and Tommy, and two sisters, Diane and Nancy. Mrs. Hazel's husband died very suddenly of a heart attack at the age of 45 while playing golf. Ronnie, at that time, was just five years old. You can imagine that this was quite a shock to Mrs. Hazel, who was widowed at an early age, with four growing children. However, Mrs. Hazel claims that having Ronnie, and realizing how much he needed her, helped her more than ever before to get through this great tragedy.

Ronnie can do so many things that our "Sunshine" cannot do. Like "Sunshine," however, one of his favorite pastimes is playing records. His collection of records is vast and he can read the names of every one. He loves TV and is a great imitator. He can read the TV Guide and knows all the shows and the times they are scheduled. His memory is very sharp and he sometimes talks about things that happened eight years ago. He reads at the fourth grade level and comprehends everything that he reads. Looking up words in the Webster Dictionary is no problem. Ronnie frequents St. Christine's, his parish church. He participates so well one would not suspect that Ronnie was retarded. He knows all the responses and prayers of the Mass. On occasions, he has served as an altar boy. Around the house, Mrs. Hazel says that Ronnie is very helpful. He can dust, use the sweeper, empty wastebaskets, keep his own bedroom clean and neat. His hygenic habits are excellent. Every night he bathes himself, washes his hair, cleans his teeth. He can even prepare for himself simple foods, such as cereal, open a can of soup and heat it, make toast, sandwiches, etc. Besides his regular curriculum in school, he is engaged in arts and crafts, swimming, gym, music, home-making which includes sewing, cooking and general housekeeping. The teacher claims he likes poetry and is good at drawing. His hand-writing is beautiful and he is good at composing sentences. He is capable of filling in blank forms regarding personal information about himself such as name, address, city and state, zip code, male or female, and telephone number. Ronnie was on a special Olympic team at school and received several awards.

When Ronnie was born, the doctor told the family that he would be a complete burden to them all his life. But as you can see from what you have just read about him, he is anything but that. All it took was love, encouragement and patience. Now Ronnie takes almost complete care of himself. On "no school days" he tells his mother to rest in bed while he makes his own breakfast. He communicates with people very nicely and carries on an intelligent conversation. But most of all, Ronnie is typical of all children with Down's Syndrome. Perhaps you are amazed at what he can do, but his most beautiful quality is his ability to love and be happy.

I believe you would enjoy reading the following letter I received from his brother Tom—"Ronnie's love is unlimited and he constantly displays it. He makes you feel wanted when he greets you, and he makes all of us feel loved. He's great to visit when you're feeling low. He displays the love people should have for each other, but are afraid to show. He is always happy, and we all envy him in so many ways."

As you can readily see, the accomplishments of "Sunshine" and Ronnie, although both mongoloids, vary so much. I have used these two children to show that retardation in the mongoloids, from my observation, is not always the same. However, one thing that they all do well and that is common to all of them is their ability to love—it is the greatest!

Schools for the retarded have a very excellent athletic program. I won't go into details with the curriculum, but if you ever have the opportunity to see a competitive sporting event that your local retarded school sponsors, by all means, don't miss it. You can take my word for it. Your eyes will bulge in amazement when you see what these children can do.

Our family looks at "Sunshine" as a unique individual without trying to compare her with other children; what she can do, or not do, is insignificant. We are very happy and fortunate to accept her just as she is. After all, our minds are still fresh with the words of our family doctor. Dr. Howard Mathay spoke to us after he completed a physical examination when she was an infant. "Mrs. Schmalzried, I don't like to tell you this, but your baby probably will never walk and will possibly be a basket-case as long as she lives."

There are many other events that have occurred in Mary Margaret's daily life not mentioned here. But what has been written will portray some concept of her progress both physically and mentally. She is loved and how her love radiates and fills the hearts of all who come in contact with her!

Touching Troubled Hearts

My sole purpose in writing my first story, *Sunshine — A Slow Miracle* ("Part One" herein), was the hope that some person with a similar situation would somehow benefit from my personal traumatic experience.

Years have passed since this original story appeared on the market. Many of its readers, particularly those faced with life's sorrows, were left with reflections that helped to influence their lives. Besides myself and the reader, a third very important party, God, was ever present—and the results were infinitely greater because of Him.

The book brought back to me favorable responses from many people, both renowned and unknown, and as far away as India. The most cherished and rewarding are the ones who gave their unsolicited testimony that the story gave them renewed courage, faith and hope to face the trials of life. I will share three of these testimonies with you.

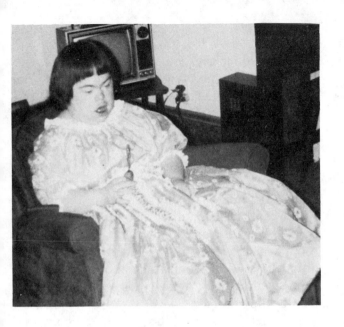

THE ANONYMOUS CALLER

After working eight hours in the office at U.S. Steel, McDonald, Ohio, I lose no time in getting home to the ones I love. I never dilly-dally on the way home. Pleasures at home are the most delightful on earth. There lies my real happiness; it is the end of almost all my pursuits and the common reward for all my labors. There is magic in that little word "home"; it is a mystic circle that surrounds comfort and virtues that are never known beyond its hallowed walls.

Alice always greets me with a loving kiss. But one day things were a little different. Although she was patiently waiting for me at the open doorway, I could see that she was excited about something, so excited, in fact, that she forgot my welcome home kiss. She was trying to tell me something about a telephone call but was talking so fast I couldn't understand all her words. I told her to calm down a bit and start over again from the very beginning.

"Oh Honey, I had the most weird, yet stimulating telephone call this afternoon about 3:30. And I can't wait to tell you about it."

We moved from the doorway into the living room where we would be more comfortable. I didn't have to question Alice about the call, for she was already in high gear as soon as we were comfortably seated.

"When I answered the phone," Alice began, "all I could hear was the sobbing of a lady's voice crying so much it was impossible for me to understand her. I was really bewildered and confused; I didn't want to break the connection, yet I felt so helpless." Alice paused for a split second to catch her breath and continued, "The crying sounded too real to be a prank, so I decided to listen a little longer."

"How long did this go on?" I interrupted.

"Oh, just about two minutes I would guess, but it seemed much longer than that."

"Did she tell you what she was crying about?" I asked.

"Yes, but I will get to that a little later. I was still having trouble trying to make any sense out of her mumbled words since she was talking and crying at the same time. Finally, she got hold of herself and gained composure; her words then began to come over the phone very clear and sweet.''

"Mrs. Schmalzried." Alice then smiled at me when she told me that the lady really had a hard time pronouncing our name.

"Yes," Alice replied.

"The lady continued, 'I just now finished reading the story your husband wrote about your retarded daughter, *Sunshine—A Slow Miracle,* and I want you people to be one of the very first to know that this story changed my entire outlook on life. It gave me the hope and strength I needed so badly to make a very important decision.'

"I replied, 'I don't quite understand. Just what is your problem if you don't mind telling me.'

" 'No, indeed,' the lady said, 'I do want to tell you, that is why I called you. During the past two years, I have had four major surgical operations and suffered severely with each. After each trip to the hospital, I was told I would be well again. Not once or twice, Mrs. Schmalzried, but four times. I became discouraged and depressed but managed somehow to keep my spirits up. But when the doctor broke the news to me that I needed a fifth operation, that was the last straw. I lost all faith in my doctor, and I was in a frame of despair. I absolutely refused to consent. I could never go through that ordeal again.' She stopped for a second and with seemingly a stronger determination of voice continued. 'My husband and our minister pleaded with me. They used all their persuasive powers to no avail. I frankly told them very emphatically, *No!*—I had had enough.'

"I sympathized with this stranger and told her, 'Surely if the operation is necessary and will restore you to good health, for your own and your family's sake, you must reconsider.' The lady seemed much happier now, almost as if I could see her smile over the phone.

" 'This is why I called,' she said, 'to tell you that after reading the story, I telephoned my husband at his office and told him to make arrangements with our doctor to schedule me for the operation as soon as possible.' "

Alice turned to me, putting her head on my shoulder and said, "Bern, I was so happy for this lady, I could almost cry, and I told her I was so thrilled that she had changed her mind. I couldn't wait to tell you about this call until you came home from work. And above all, I told her that we would remember her in our prayers.

"Then her voice sounded like it choked up a little, 'Thanks, Mrs. Schmalzried.' I appreciate your patience with me and your kind indulgence in hearing me out. I just had to tell you all about my problem. And please give "Sunshine" a big hug and kiss for giving me the courage I needed to carry on.'

"I replied, 'I certainly will do that right away.' And with that we both bid each other goodbye."

Frankly, I was stunned with the facts of this event. To think that our little retarded one had the influence to perform such an act of mercy.

"Did the lady make known her physical ailment? And did she give her name, or where she lived?" I asked.

"No, she never mentioned anything about her identity or her whereabouts, and I did not think I should ask her. I thought if she wanted me to know, surely she would have told me."

To this day, we have no idea who this caller was, or if the fifth operation was a success. But, we do know that our retarded child was instrumental in giving her new hope to continue on in life.

This story of the anonymous caller alone proves that the retarded and handicapped are not useless, but rather have an important mission for society. God gave them a special way of influencing people. The more I see of the handicapped, the more I am convinced that God turns "evil" into good by enlarging our hearts. He makes us unselfish and fills us with kindly sympathies and affections. He gives our souls higher aims. He calls out all our faculties to

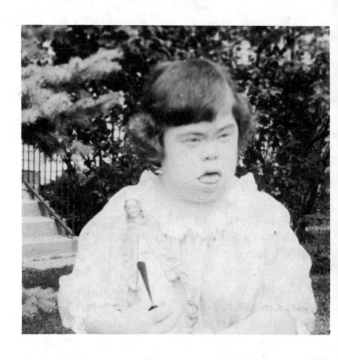

extended enterprise and exertions. To sum it all up, I think God calls upon the handicapped to be His messengers. He sends them forth, day by day, to tell us of love, hope and peace.

UNFOUNDED GUILT

When the story of *Sunshine — A Slow Miracle* was published, it never occurred to me that I would be receiving mail from both near and far. My blindness to this fact is the reason that I was puzzled when I received the very first such letter bearing an unfamiliar postmark—Santa Ana, California—dated October 25, 1966. However, I lost no time in opening the envelope, and to my surprise it was from a stranger—a young mother who was torturing herself with a sense of guilt because she gave birth to a handicapped child. She saw in me, through the story, a father who personally experienced tragedy and hurt, and who successfully overcame this bitter, torturous path of thorns that came into my life. She, too, wanted desperately to shed the yoke of sadness and live again a normal life in peace and with a clear conscience. She was reaching out to me, asking for my help.

My first reaction after reading the letter was one of elation. I was excited that this young mother thought so much of my traumatic experience that she would take time out from her busy day to write to me. As you read her letter, you will see that she stated some parts of the book helped her very much, but wanted to further communicate with me to ease her mind in areas not mentioned in the story. At that moment, I was most anxious to get busy and answer her.

But then, momentarily, I had second thoughts about all this. Why should I take time to reply? This lady is a stranger to me, over 3,000 miles away, a person I had never met and no doubt never would. Besides, if she is mentally troubled, she should seek professional help. What could I offer to give her some relief? The devil in my mind continued to haunt me with these negative thoughts—certainly not Christ-like thoughts. "If I start to correspond with this stranger, will she become a nuisance? What will I gain by answering her? Everybody has some kind of problems. I solved mine; let her find her own answers. Why should I get involved?" At this precise moment, the word *involved* acted like a brake spinning the wheels in my head to a complete stop and reversing my train of thought to a more positive stance. "Isn't this a very common expression we hear so often today?—I would have helped, or I would have done this or that, but I didn't want to get *involved*. How inconsiderate I am when I am so fortunate and blessed with so many good things in life that I should turn my back on the cries of my less fortunate fellowman. Have I forgotten so easily that if not for the grace of God I could be the unfortunate one again?"

Why I hesitated for a split second to answer this cry for hope was just plain selfishness on my part. I really knew better; my built-in alarm system, called a conscience, told me just what my obligations were. I was aware also that those who are not selfish have the best ammunition for being happy. But I guess my human frailty in seeking the easy way out tried to take command. However, the teachings of Jesus Christ so proudly and patiently taught me by my widowed mother in my childhood, and by my Church in later years, were not wasted.

The lessons that Jesus gave the world during His three years of ministry gave me many beneficial guidelines on how to live a more peaceful life within myself and with my neighbor. The teachings that Jesus preached were not intended to reach just the ears of the people of His day, but rather were for all future generations until the end of time. In His wisdom, He inspired the authors of Sacred Scripture to record His teachings, and entrusted the Church He founded to preserve and spread the Word to peoples of every nation.

The Holy Bible contains immeasurable wealth of material for our spiritual well-being. But the lesson I believe that is most fitting at this point in time is the beautiful story of the Good Samaritan. I am sure that all Christians are familiar with this story of love as told in Luke 10:25-37. It is the story of a certain lawyer who was trying to test Jesus and asked what he should do to be saved. Jesus answered him by telling him to "Love the Lord your God with your whole heart, and with your whole mind; and with your whole soul; with your whole strength; and your neighbor as yourself." But the lawyer inquired—" 'Who is my neighbor?' Jesus replied: 'There was a man going down from Jerusalem to Jericho who fell prey to robbers. They stripped him, beat him, and then went off leaving him half-dead. A priest happened to be going down the same road; he saw him but continued on.

Mary Connor and her family—1974

Likewise there was a Levite who came the same way; he saw him and went on. But a Samaritan who was journeying along came on him and was moved to pity at the sight. He approached him and dressed his wounds, pouring in oil and wine. He then hoisted him on his own beast and brought him to an inn, where he cared for him. The next day he took out two silver pieces and gave them to the innkeeper with the request: "Look after him, and if there is any further expense I will repay you on my way back."

'Which of these three, in your opinion, was neighbor to the man who fell in with the robbers?' The answer came, 'The one who treated him with compassion.' Jesus said to him, 'Then go and do the same' " (Lk. 10:29-37).

In the Bible story, the man was badly beaten by robbers and left along the roadside to die—and probably would have died if the Good Samaritan had not happened to come along. But there are many different ways that our neighbor may be hurt and suffering. Do we see his plight and ignore it like the priest and Levite, or do we offer our help like the Good Samaritan?

As you read the following letter from Mrs. C. Connor, you will notice there was no physical violence, but nevertheless the need for another person's support was evident, if for no other reason than just to talk to a person who has already felt the sting of sorrow. She believed that I would understand her sorrow readily and vividly, and offer some antidote for her troubled mind.

October—, 19—

Dear Mr. Schmalzried, "Sunshine" and Family:

After reading your book, *A Slow Miracle*, I wanted very much to write to you and say what a truly lovely story it is. Your little "Sunshine" is a darling, and I wanted her to have this medal. It is very precious and has quite a story behind it—at any rate I want "Sunshine" to have it.

My name is Mary Connor, and I have four sons, one of whom has a multiple handicap. His name is "Jay Michael," age four, and very precious to us. He has cerebral palsy and is not walking as of now, but we have much hope and faith. As a result the palsy has left him with poor eyesight, also some mental retardation, and he was born with an open heart. In spite of all this he is doing well, and has such a loving disposition.

I have prayed very hard, but do not accept this as I should. I find it so difficult at times. Please pray for me that I too can receive this slow miracle from God. I also have such a guilty feeling about Jay as he was born two months early as I overdid when we moved. I want very much to receive your attitude and understanding. Please pray for me.

When I find it very hard, I will read parts of your book, which helped me very much.

Please tell "Sunshine" hello for us, and I am enclosing a picture of Jay for her.

Please answer when you get a chance. And thanks for your story.

Sincerely,
Mary Connor

After reading the letter again and again, each word sank deeper into my mind and heart. I didn't know this woman, but still she was no longer a stranger—she was my neighbor. In my mind's eye, I could picture her as she wrote this letter. I saw her as a young, loving mother whose face was drawn with worry and sadness. Her complexion is pallid, and a tear finds its way down her cheek and plops down onto her writing paper. I see her tears as messengers of overwhelming grief, and of unspeakable love for her handicapped son. My heart ached for her; I wanted to reach out to her and comfort her, but I felt so inadequate—what could I do, what could I say? Surely I didn't have the answers, but I turned to our heavenly Father and petitioned Him to guide me.

November—, 19—

Dear Mrs. Connor:

I was very surprised and happy that you thought so much of my story, "Sunshine," to take time to write to me. I was sorry to learn of your problems but was overjoyed that the story had helped you so much. I will be glad to correspond with you; I only pray that I will be able to say something that will clear your mind of what I believe is unfounded guilt and somehow help you acquire a better acceptance of Jay's condition. I am no expert on giving advice, but my experience may be of some help to you.

The great love that mothers have for their children is something God gave to them as a special gift. I dearly love all my children, but a mother's love is different. No language can ever begin to express the power and beauty and heroism and majesty of a mother's love. This great, deep gift of love that you have for Jay, and even greater due to his affliction, could be the primary reason for your guilt feeling. For when we love somebody so dearly, we surely don't want to hurt him or see him suffer. Therefore, due to the absence of medical explanation for Jay's condition, you blamed yourself.

However, Alice also possesses this exceptional mother's love. When "Sunshine" was born, she pondered a little on this subject, for when she was just a few months pregnant, she engaged in some strenuous painting in the living room. She thought perhaps the fumes from the paint might have had some effect on the baby's condition. But when she questioned Dr. Allan Altdoerffer, he assured her that the paint absolutely did not have any ill-effect on the baby. Fortunately, Alice accepted his word and dismissed the thought from her mind.

Luckily, I never was bothered with any guilt feeling. I was ever so thankful that I had had five wonderful, good, healthy children prior to "Sunshine." And every time I looked at one of my children, I marveled at the mysterious, miraculous, creative power of God. I see the little, perfectly formed body, the little legs and arms with their tiny toes and fingers, the ears, the mouth, nose, eyes and hair. Then there are the inner functional parts, the brain, heart, liver, digestive system and all the others, too numerous to mention. All these perfectly formed in just nine months. It is beyond me how any intelligent person can deny there is a God when the proof is strongly evident. I must believe all this creation had an intelligent beginning, that Someone made it happen. I cannot accept the proposition that at random points in time, such entities as intelligence, personality, memory and the entire human body just sort of fell together.

Mary, the development of the baby from the moment of conception to birth staggers my little brain; but I don't feel bad about this, since even great scientific minds don't know all the answers. But all this beautiful formation of the baby, we know, is very mysterious and complex. Think about this for just a minute. Isn't it reasonable to think that nature could make a mistake once in awhile? Then, when something does go haywire, and there is nothing we can do about it, many times we look around to blame someone or blame ourselves. Why haunt the doctors for answers and cures? We might waylay our pastors with the questions, "What have I done to deserve this?" We even sometimes blame God and turn away from Him instead of reaching for His outstretched hands. All these radical make-up remedies have but one result. They make everybody more miserable and only add to our difficulties without solving a thing.

From my experience with "Sunshine," the answer lies in total acceptance. Acceptance is the only real source of tranquillity, serenity and peace. It can be acquired only if one has the urgent desire to help oneself, and to ask God for His help. I also found that the Serenity Prayer has been of some help to me. I hope you find it equally beneficial. "God, grant me the serenity to accept the things I cannot change; the courage to change the things I can; and the wisdom to know the difference."

Sure, I asked myself the popular question, "Why does God permit this evil?" It took me a little longer to understand, and maybe I don't even completely comprehend, but I know that God is all-good and has a great love for me. He does not condone evil, but permits it; and with His help, we can turn evil around to perform some good. I found this to be so true with "Sunshine." I just cannot express the good she has done, not only for me and my family, but for so many others, and countless numbers who have been helped by her, through the book *Sunshine.* So when you find yourself in a seemingly hopeless situation, you must not rebel. You must believe that God has His reasons, in His infinite goodness and wisdom, for permitting it. And, Mary, when you fully understand this and accept your cross by saying, "Thy will be done," almost immediately the load of guilt will vanish from your mind, and assurance that all will work out for the better brings with it peace of mind.

I found life to be thickly sown with thorns, and the best remedy that I found was to pass as quickly as possible through them. The longer we dwell on our misfortunes, the greater is their power to do us some harm. There are times when things are so bad, one thing after another befalls us; we are tempted to think that God demands misery and suffering in this life. This is far from the truth. God wants us to be happy, and He even shows us the way (the lessons in the Bible). I used to think that happiness consisted in fulfillment of my wants and desires, or in freedom from pain and suffering, but I now know that happiness consists in serenity that comes from loving God and conforming my will to His.

In the early days of "Sunshine's" life, when I looked at her retarded condition and thought of her bleak future in this society, I suffered—she didn't suffer; it was I. And this turned out to be good for me. This proved to be the perfect tool to open my eyes to the real values of life and bring me closer to God, so that I got to know Him better and consequently love Him more. The way of the cross may be difficult, but it remains the only sure way to happiness and peace in this life. And when this life ends, there awaits happiness without measure, without limit, without end.

Mary, by this time you probably are sorry that you wrote to me. You never expected such a long reply. I hope I didn't tire you or bore you. But when you asked me for my attitude, I did not want to miss anything, although I am sure I have not covered everything, and besides, when anybody asks about "Sunshine," I can sing her praises forever.

Your precious Jay, like Sunshine, has a special mission assigned to no other person. But he cannot do it himself; he needs your help. Whatever you do, please do not cuddle or shelter Jay from your neighbors. The handicapped have a way of making Christ's presence known to everyone, even the hard-core doubters. Perhaps you have already noticed in your family the strong bond of love that Jay has brought with him. Love is his mission—the family is only the beginning; open your front door and let his love find its way through city streets. Maybe you are not aware of it, but Jay is one of God's apostles who in his own way will bring sheep to the Shepherd.

And remember, Mary, the happiest, sweetest, tenderest homes are not those where there has been no sorrow, but those which have been overshadowed with grief, and where Christ's comfort was accepted.

I sincerely hope that I didn't say anything in this letter to offend you, but rather I pray that you will find a little something that will be helpful to you. Please feel welcome to write as often as you want. If there are any questions you would like to ask, please do not hesitate. You can see from the length of this letter that I do not mind writing.

God bless you and your family.

Sincerely,

B. R. Schmalzried, Sr.

I realized that my letter was lengthy, but I wanted to make certain that I covered all areas that I thought would help her. Even after I mailed the letter, I was exploring my mind for a little something of importance that I might have overlooked.

Our correspondence did not end here. Through the years we exchanged letters, pertaining for the most part to the progress being made by both Jay and "Sunshine." The next letter I received from Santa Ana, Mrs. Connor seemed to be happier. She also told me in that letter that a troop of boy scouts took Jay to Disneyland for a full day. In still a later note, she told me that they had had Jay admitted to a day school that accepted multi-handicapped children. Later she wrote:

Thank you for your wonderful letters. They have helped me so much, as did your book. My one wish now is that Jay will walk. I now realize God has been good to me. My biggest problem was the terrible guilt feeling I had.

I now quote from a letter with a December date:

"We have taken in two foster boys, ages three and four. Both have Down's Syndrome. They are darling;

Mary Connor and Jay—1978

we had Ronnie since the first of April and Kenny just since the first of November. My boys just love them and they all get along so well. With six boys, we never have a dull moment."

In conclusion, Jay's leg was operated on, and later he had the other leg operated on. He can now walk with the aid of braces.

When Jay was 18, Mrs. Connor wrote:

Jay is now 18 and really a joy. He's always interested in others and what they have to say. He has excellent hearing, but poor eyesight, for he is blind in one eye and sees very little out of the other. He has all the patience in the world and never, never complains.

He is a real sports fan and knows every player and his position whether it's football, baseball or basketball. God has given him such a knowledge and understanding of these sports that they help him pass the time. He goes to a special school for the handicapped and is well liked by the students and teachers.

A big part of Jay's life had been my father, Joseph Liebold, until he passed away last June. They had had such a special relationship. If it had not been for Dad and Mom, those early years after Jay was born, it would have been much harder. They would come over to help me out, and then take Jay with them over weekends and give him all their special attention. Mom lives with us now, and we all love her and appreciate all she and Dad did for us.

Our two foster sons with Down's Syndrome and Jay have been accepted by our other sons—Roger, Jeff, Dean, and Andrew. We thank God for them all. Each one is so special.

When you see the love and patience our handicapped boys have, you certainly see God in them. You know that God gave them to you for a special reason. All the children have made our family closer and helped us realize we are here to serve our Lord on this earth and do *His* will the best we can.

I can honestly say that through all the difficult times, and they were many, God was right with us, carrying us through it all. I recall the time I received a telephone call from the Foundation for the Junior Blind in Los Angeles years ago, asking me if I would like Jay to go to their summer camp. Chuck and I said "yes." For six years Jay went to their camp, where the teachers were so devoted and kind to him. That telephone call was truly God's doing!

That's all for now, Bernie and Alice.

Love to all. Give "Sunshine" a big kiss for us.

Mary, Chuck, and all the Connors

It was very rewarding to both Alice and I, that our retarded daughter was influential in helping Mrs. Connor overcome her guilt feeling. The successful outcome of this true story belongs entirely to "Sunshine," since without her existence no book would have been published, and Mrs. Connor would never have written that first letter to me.

"IF THERE IS ROOM IN THE HEART..."

This precious story, as it unfolds, will reveal to you the wonderful mysterious work-

ings of God's great love. (The name of the
parents has been changed to avoid publicity.)
It all began one quiet Wednesday evening with
a telephone call about 9:00 p.m. I was surprised and happy to hear the voice of a dear
friend of the family, Reverend John Spitale.
Father had been assistant pastor at St. Rose
and was now doing God's work for the people
in Holy Rosary parish in Lowellville. After the
usual pleasant greetings, Father got to the purpose of his call immediately.

"Bernie, I just arrived home from North
Side Hospital. I spent the entire evening
visiting a member of my parish, a Mrs. Ruth
Tor. She gave birth to a mongoloid baby last
Sunday."

"Yes," I interrupted Father just to let him
know I was listening.

"Well, this young lady is only in her twen-
ties and it's her first child."

"That's a shame," I mentioned to Father,
"but I guess this is one of those exceptional
cases."

"The reason I called," Father seemed to be
anxious to get on with the problem, "this mother
will not have anything to do with this baby. The
husband has mixed emotions about the child, but
will do whatever his wife wants to do. The doc-

tor suggested that the baby be sent directly from the hospital to an institution. He claims that these children cannot be trained, nothing can be done for them, and would create only undue hardship for the entire family. And to make matters even worse, Ruth's mother agrees with the doctor one hundred percent."

"That's too bad," I countered in a sad voice.

"Yes, I agree," said Father, "but Ruth cannot think clearly for herself. She is in a state of frustration and confusion, depressed and inconsolable. I could not get to first base with her. No matter what I said, it was like there was a brick wall between us. I was just not getting through. I tried to use all my priestly experience and theology and philosophy and everything I could think of. It was one of those rare times in my life when I felt that I had completely struck out.

"Then I thought of how wonderfully you and Alice, in fact, your entire family, accepted your mongoloid baby. And maybe you or Alice could come to the hospital and talk to Ruth."

"We would love to, but what does Mrs. Tor say about this?" I questioned.

"Oh, I told her and her husband all about you and your family, and she said that you could come in and visit with her. I at least was successful in selling her on that idea."

"That sounds good, Father. I will talk this over with Alice right away and I am sure she will agree to do whatever we can. I'll call you back and keep you informed. By the way, Father, do you have Ruth's room number?"

"Yes, Bernie, she is in Room 202, and good luck. I'll flood heaven with prayers for your success."

With this, we bid each other goodbye for the present.

Alice sensed that this was an untimely telephone call and she was curious to know what it was all about. I was as anxious to tell her. So, I lost no time in filling her in with all the details from beginning to end. Alice agreed with me that when a situation like this arises, one feels so insecure or inadequate.

"What does Father think we can do—it seems to me, from what you told me, she already has her mind made up."

"That's true, but what can we lose? All we can do is talk to her as parents who have had the same experience. Remember when Dr. Altdoerffer told us, 'If you have love in your hearts for this baby, you will find room in your home.' Perhaps we might say something like that. It could be just a little thing like that that could change her mind."

"It's worth a try," Alice said. "Let's tell Father that we will go tomorrow night."

I lost no time in telephoning Father and told him that we agreed to talk to Mr. and Mrs. Tor the following evening, which was Thursday. I told Father to keep the prayers flowing.

What could we say, what could we do? If Father failed, what chance would we have to be successful? These thoughts raced through my mind all day Thursday, and I am sure Alice was bothered with the same troublesome questions. As the time approached for visiting hours, we gathered together all the information we had on "Sunshine"—anything and everything that we thought would be of some help.

First, there was a portrait of "Sunshine." A magazine article featured in *St. Ann's Annals;* a story in our local newspaper, *The Girard News,* and also *The Catholic Exponent;* and a copy of the manuscript, *Sunshine—A Slow Miracle.* At this time, the story was in the hands of the publisher, but not yet released. We really wanted to take "Sunshine" in person, but hospital rules forbade it.

On the way to the hospital, Alice suggested that since it was a maternity ward, she thought it best if she made the visit alone. I agreed wholeheartedly. And now I could relax! Besides, I believed Alice could talk mother to mother much better without me. So I stayed in the car, shut off the radio, and began to say a few rosaries that everything would work out for the best.

Alice's visit lasted a good hour or more, and you can imagine how curious I was to learn what took place. When I saw Alice coming up the walk towards our parked car, I ran part way to meet her. She was not smiling and appeared to be disappointed. Her first words to me were very disheartening.

"Hon, I failed. I didn't do any good."

By this time, I was opening the car door for Alice and I said, "You can tell me about it on the way home."

As we pulled out of the parking lot, Alice commenced to tell me about her visit:

"Evidently, Father Spitale called to tell Mrs. Tor and her husband to expect us. I knocked on the partly opened door and walked into the room. Mrs. Tor was in the far end of the room. The other bed was unoccupied. Mrs. Tor's husband was standing alongside her bed handing his wife a glass of ice water. As I walked towards her, I introduced myself.

'' 'Mrs. Tor, I am Alice Schmalzried. Father Spitale told me about your baby and asked me if I would pay you a visit.'

'' 'Yes, Father did tell me about you and your family, but no matter what you say, you won't change my mind,' she said in a very determined and hostile voice.

'' 'Oh, pardon me, do you want me to leave?' I replied as I took a step backward.

" 'No, no, you may stay, but I have definitely decided that my baby will not go home with me. I am already making arrangements with an institution to take care of her.'

"Inasmuch as the air was a little on the chilly side, I decided to change the subject and talk about the weather and my other five children. The change seemed to work wonders. Mrs. Tor became more relaxed and friendly with me. She enjoyed hearing about our son, Bernie, who was in the seminary studying to be a priest and our daughter, Maureen, who was also away studying to enter the religious life as a Daughter of Charity. I never did get around to telling about Bobby, Albert or Jimmy, as I thought the time was now ripe to try again to get back on the subject of mongoloid babies. My assumption was correct, for when I began to talk about "Sunshine," Ruth was more receptive and asked a lot of questions. As Ruth and I talked, Mr. Tor reached over and picked up the picture of "Sunshine" and asked, 'I can't believe that this is a mongoloid child. Are all mongoloids this beautiful?'

"I believe that Mr. Tor had a warped image of what a mongoloid child looked like and when he saw "Sunshine's" picture with her radiant smile, he was surprised. I smiled as I looked at him and answered, 'Why certainly, all mongoloid children are beautiful. Of course, I think "Sunshine" is the prettiest because she is mine and she even looks like me.'

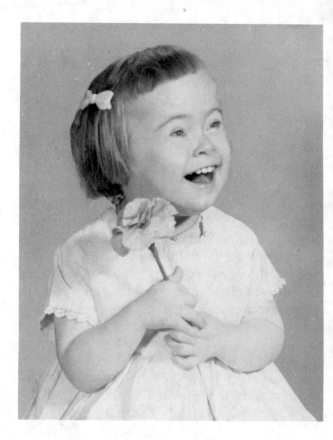

'' 'She is pretty,' he said as he shook his head in a surprised gesture.

''At this moment, just when the conversation was going well and I thought I was making some headway, who came into the room but the grandmother!

''After the usual introductions, the subject of retarded children again filled the air. When I

mentioned that the mongoloids were very pleasant and never known to be violent or vicious (we
learned this from our pediatrician, Dr. Allan Altdoerffer), the grandmother interrupted,

" 'I disagree with you, Mrs. Schmalzried; we
have a retarded child in our neighborhood and
he is vicious. He is always fighting with the other
children.' (She didn't say if the child was brain-
damaged or mongoloid and I didn't ask.)

" 'Do the other neighborhood children tease
him?' I inquired.

"At this point, Mr. Tor spoke up.

" 'Yes, Mom, the other children are always
teasing Jimmy. I guess that is why he gets mad
and scraps with them.'

" 'Sure, if the retarded child fights back
when he is teased, he is called vicious,' I replied.
'But if a normal child fights back under the same
circumstances, it's considered all right.'

"At this point, the grandmother said no more
but picked up her visitor's card to see the baby
and slowly departed from the room. I told Ruth
that I would love to see the baby also, and she
cheerfully handed me the other ticket that was
on the night stand. As I made my exit from the
room, I had the feeling that the purpose of my
visit was a complete failure. However, as I
walked down the hall towards the viewing window, I said a few silent, quick prayers to the
Holy Spirit that He might guide me to the right
words that would change Ruth's mind. Ruth's

mother was walking very slowly and I soon caught up with her. However, I didn't get a chance to say anything as she totally ignored the conversation by repeating that institutionalizing the baby was the best thing to do for all concerned.

''The baby happened to be in the crib in the very first row next to the big window. I got a real good look at the unwanted infant, and to me, she was really a doll. I would have just loved to hold and cuddle her in my arms. I cannot begin to tell you how sweet and beautiful she was. On my slow journey back to Room 202, I was thinking to myself what a shame that this little innocent creature was classed as a reject, a mistake of nature. She does not belong in an institution. All she needs is tender loving care and she would bring joy to this family if only given the chance.

''The grandmother was already in the room when I entered. I ignored everyone else in the room and went to Ruth's bedside and told her what a lovely baby she had and how I wished that she were mine. I then looked straight into Ruth's eyes and said with a very sincere and firm voice, 'Ruth, I'll tell you what I'll do. You take this baby home with you and keep her for six months. If after six months you decide you don't want her, and I mean this, *I will take her and adopt her.'*

" 'No matter what you do or say, Mrs. Schmalzried, you will never change my mind,' she repeated.

"At this time, I realized that I had done all I could. I left the manuscript and the other material with her. I departed with a cheery goodbye and wished luck to all, but inside my heart was heavy. I had failed as badly as Father Spitale, but I had done my best and God knows that I tried, which is all that He expects of us."

We were just about home when Alice finished telling me about the hospital visit. I, too, was disappointed with the results of her endeavors and my mind was now trying to find answers. If only they would give the baby a chance as Alice suggested. But no, the influence and respect for their family doctor's advice was a very definite deciding factor, I thought. If we had had the same doctor when "Sunshine" was born and he had told us to institutionalize our baby, what would we have done? I don't mean to say that in some cases institutionalizing is not the proper answer. Some families just could not cope with raising a retarded child. In such cases, it would not be good for the child, nor the family. But, in our case, we were fortunate to have a doctor who was more knowledgeable about what *could be done* for these children, and who also had done a little checking and knew that the family could accept this baby with love.

When we arrived home, our children—
Bobby, Albert and Jimmy—were still awake.
We told them the whole story, or as much of it
as we thought they would understand. Alice told
them how sweet the baby was and how she was
just like their little sister, "Sunshine." We also
told them that if the mother did not want her, we
might bring her home with us and keep her. This
made them very excited and happy. They went
to bed that night elated because they envisioned
getting another baby sister just like "Sunshine"
whom they loved so dearly.

After they were tucked snugly into bed, we
wrote letters to both Maureen and Bernie. We
explained our experience in detail to them and
asked them to remember the Tor family in their
prayers. It was not too late to phone our good
friend, Father Spitale, for we knew he would be
very interested. Even though we admitted
failure, Father could not begin to thank us
enough for taking the time to visit Ruth. Later,
Father confirmed his thanks and appreciation to
us in a letter thus:

I was deeply move by Alice's attitude. She could
have easily shrugged the whole thing off and said, "I
have enough problems of my own." But it was a
beautiful thing for her to go and offer herself in that
way and try to bring some light and comfort. It was a
lift for me as a priest just to know I could call on
someone like that.

Alice and I prayed for the Tor family that they might make the right decision. From Friday on, our children persistently asked us if we would get the baby. The pressure from the children built up so intensely that by Sunday noon, Alice decided to get them off her back, so she called the hospital. She asked for Room 202-A and a nurse who just happened to be in the room at the time answered the telephone. Alice identified herself and asked if Mrs. Tor was available.

"No, Mrs. Tor was discharged yesterday," came the professional but courteous reply.

"Could you tell me if she took the baby home with her or placed her in an institution?" Alice quickly questioned and held her breath —hoping, hoping, hoping the answer would be what we had prayed so hard for.

"Yes, she decided to take the baby home with her," came the welcome good news.

Upon hearing this good news you might try to imagine the joy that raced through Alice's heart. Usually great joy, especially after a sudden change of circumstances, is apt to be silent, and dwells rather in the heart than on the tongue. But this news was different, our entire family was involved and was to share in this happiness. After thanking the nurse, and placing the telephone gently on the table, Alice lost no time in rushing to us breathlessly to give us the glad tidings.

The children were very disappointed. But when we explained to them how much better it would be for the baby to be with her own Mom and Daddy, they understood and were completely satisfied.

About seven weeks passed and we never heard another word from the Tors. You might try to appreciate how apprehensive Alice and I were during this period of time. Our minds were fumbling with questions.

Then on the seventh week of anxiety, when we returned from a weekend visit with our daughter Maureen, in Emmitsburg, Maryland, we noticed our mailbox was stuffed with a large brown envelope. The return address on this first-class postage revealed the name of Mrs. Tor. When I saw this name, I lost no time in opening the door and hastily turned on the lights in the living room. As I opened the envelope Alice and all the children were circled around me, anxious as I was to learn of its contents. The package contained all the literature Alice had left with Mrs. Tor at the hospital: the manuscript, the pictures and newspaper clippings of "Sunshine." But the prize was the beautiful handwritten letter that Mrs. Tor personally wrote. I consider this letter a masterpiece revealing a heart full of love. The letter I still have in my possession and I will cherish it always.

I would like to mention at this time that for all the hours I put into writing, I never realized one penny for my work. I requested all profits from the sale of my book be used by the Daughters of St. Paul to help them in their apostolate in spreading the Word of God. But this one letter alone was worth more to me than all the gold in the vaults in Fort Knox. As I read it, tears blotted my vision. I was helpless to stop the flow of moisture that so freely and uncontrollably flowed down my cheeks. I was not embarrassed by this display of affection in the presence of my family because these were tears of joy.

Dear Mr. and Mrs. Schmalzried,

I am at long last returning your stories about your precious "Sunshine." I'm sorry I haven't returned it sooner. Your story is so much like our own. I must tell you that I appreciated your visit to me in the hospital very much. I stayed up that very night till past midnight reading your story. I couldn't begin to tell you how deeply touched I was. Well, I didn't actually accept my baby until the day before I was to leave the hospital. And do you remember when you told me that I would change my mind and I said I wouldn't? You told me that in six months if I didn't want her that you would take her; well, hardly two months have passed and I wouldn't trade her for the world. She is the most beautiful baby you've ever seen. She's such a good baby for us and she is so pleasant. Of course, I know it will be a little harder as time goes by, but right now, she's just as any other baby would be, but a little more precious. My husband took to her right away, but to me, she's a little more special.

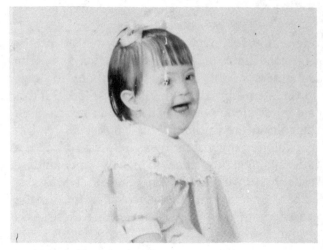

Cynthia Angel Tor, 2 years old

My priest, Father Witt, has just left my home after blessing our baby and left me your published book. I will always go back and read it if at some time I'm not sure about something. I know that your "Sunshine" must be very dear to you as my little "Angel" is to me. For you see, I called her "Cynthia Angel," for I felt that's just what she was, an "Angel" of God sent just to people like you and me. So, now, we have something in common ("Sunshine" and "Angel"). Two special creatures from heaven. God bless you and your whole family.

Ruth Tor

The letter was the answer to our prayers. Our hearts were no longer heavy with the weight of defeat, but rather lifted to the heights of untold gladness.

The beautiful ending to the story does not end with the letter. About sixteen months quickly sped by and we heard not another word from the Tors. Then by accident one day, Alice met Ruth with her retarded baby and the grandmother while shopping at the Youngstown Liberty Plaza on Belmont Avenue. Both Ruth and the grandmother were as proud as peacocks as they introduced "Cynthia Angel" to just about every salesclerk in the store.

What great happiness this child brought to this family by giving her the chance to love and be loved! What sorrow would still exist if this child had been institutionalized.

This example, in addition to those that have been written or which have not been written, and possibly countless others not known to me, are testimonies of Mary Margaret's important mission here on earth. How can any person now truthfully say that "Sunshine" and all the other handicapped persons' lives are a waste and no value to society?

The Value of the Human Person

It is not what a man has, or even what he accomplishes, which expresses his true value.

Sunshine, captain of the poontoon boat at Canadahta Lake—1978

Man himself is the crowning wonder of all creation, and every individual has his own beauty. In each person there is a proper and peculiar charm. Therefore, we should not look at man as merely a production unit, but rather as the most wonderful of all creations and the child of God. Every soul is of infinite value and is immortal. But, often in our quest for worldly things we overlook this richest treasure of them all—the human person.

Therefore, it is good that certain things take place periodically to remind us of these truths. One such occasion took place on July 1, 1979, at a Commencement Program for the graduating class at the Mahoning County School for the Mentally Retarded, in Youngstown, Ohio. The main address was given by my son, the Reverend Bernard R. Schmalzried, Pastoral Administer, Cardinal Mooney High School, Youngstown, Ohio.

The twenty-three children of the graduating class were as happy as any children, in any school, finishing their elementary classes. There would be a slight difference, however. Instead of advancing into high school, these children would be assigned to the school's workshop. They looked upon this promotion with much excitement, joy and anticipation. The following year, they would be taught to make many beautiful and useful items. The children with the broader learning abilities would even learn a trade which would give them the opportunity to contribute to their own support in the future.

The auditorium was overflowing with parents, relatives, friends and neighbors. I arrived a little late and had to be satisfied with standing room next to the wall. However, from this vantage point I had an excellent view of the entire hall. My eyes became fixed, for the most part, on the parents. And my mind was trying to diagnose, from their facial expressions, just what their attitudes were regarding this graduation. I could not see into their hearts, but as a father with a retarded child, I was concerned. Would this program once again activate the deep wounds of sorrow that they had so successfully smothered through the years by their love and affection? In their mind's eyes did they see their babies, so dependent on them for just about everything, growing so fast into adulthood without the necessary tools of intelligence to be accepted and successful in this cold, competitive world? Were they tempted to cry out once again, "Lord, why did this happen to me"? In spite of their great parental love, did they show any signs of tears, sorrow, or resentment?

If any of the parents or, in fact, any person in the hall harbored such thoughts, I could not detect them. Truly, this was a very happy gathering of people that came to celebrate a very touching and solemn occasion. But, if anyone held any doubts or fears for the worth of these children, their minds were set at ease when the words of the main address reached their ears.

This speech had such a profound effect upon every person in the auditorium that I was very anxious to obtain a copy of the address so others might profit from the words of truth and wisdom that it contained. Without a doubt it enlightened our minds and brought into focus the value of the human person in a way that most of us never thought of before. This speech was the highlight of this beautiful program and I feel privileged to be able to present it to my readers.

I realize that a printed speech is like a dried flower; the substance, indeed, is there, but the color is faded and the perfume is gone. But, in spite of the fact that you cannot have the prerogative of hearing the speaker's voice, or seeing his many timely and appropriate facial expressions and gestures, I am sure that you will enjoy, profit from, and cherish the valuable reflections it conveys. And this is particularly true for all the persons whose loved ones are afflicted with a handicap.

The Speech

Hundreds of miles to the west of us, in the state of South Dakota, a colossal project is nearing completion. A man named Korczak Ziolkowski single-handedly began this project about thirty years ago. He had the dream of sculpturing the side of a mountain. When he finishes his work, Korczak Ziolkowski will stand back and admire a monument to the Sioux Indian Chief, Crazy Horse. The statue will depict the Sioux Chief riding his horse as in battle and giving directions to his followers with one arm pointing confidently in the direction of the challenge.

The monument being carved, drilled and blasted from the side of Thunderhead Mountain is huge! It stands 641 feet long, 513 feet high, larger than the heads of the American Presidents on Mount Rushmore.

During the past thirty years, Korczak Ziolkowski has given his life to his project, and has nearly lost his life in the process. While drilling and blasting and moving tons of rock he has broken his arms and his back; he broke a leg and still walks with a limp; he has fractured his ribs; he has suffered two heart attacks; he has lost most of his hearing. And yet, at the age of seventy, he is more determined than ever to complete his project.

The work of Mr. Ziolkowski has attracted world-wide attention. Each summer a million tourists stop at the work-site to view the statue's progress. Three years ago, I was among them. Millions more will view the monument and its picture will, in all likelihood, become as famous as the postcards of Mount Rushmore. A thousand years from now the statue of the Indian-on-a-Horse might inspire the same wonder as the Egyptian Pyramids, not for its engineering feat, but for the desire and dedication of a single individual.

I do not wish to discredit the work of Korczak Ziolkowski. I admire his self-sacrifice, hard work, and especially his recognition of a neglected and suppressed people, the American Indians. I hope that his monument will be seen and appreciated by millions of people for thousands of years. The monument will do a lot of good in our own time if it helps to rekindle a spirit of pride in our native Americans.

I honestly believe, however, that what we are celebrating tonight—the commencement of these young men and women—is a much more beautiful and significant accomplishment.

—The Crazy Horse Monument should soon be finished and, except for the erosion of its features, it will stand unchanged for centuries. It will be *finished*. The lives of these young adults are not finished, not completed. Tonight's ceremony marks a step in their development. They will continue to learn, to work and to grow. As the years pass, they will continue to develop their human personalities and their God-given potential. Using the opportunities available to them, and building upon experience, they will become better and more beautiful persons.

—The Crazy Horse Monument is a colossal statue to the American past. These graduates remind us that the education of young people, the interest shown them, and the opportunities provided for their development are the best assurance of America's future. These young men and women will touch the lives of other people. They will contribute to the American way of life through the work they do, through the relationships they maintain, and through the personal qualities they have.

—The Crazy Horse Monument is an image in rock. The young people we honor tonight have been created in the image of God. Their personalities are unique because each one of them manifests a special aspect of God's creative goodness. They remind us that although there are billions of people in the world, and there have been billions in ages past, and there will be billions more, God does not mass-produce. Each human life is His special handiwork, dearly loved by Him.

—The Crazy Horse Monument, for all its artistic qualities and despite its magnificence, cannot bring one ray of human love or one degree of human warmth into the lives of other people. These young men and women have brought and will continue to bring, smiles of appreciation to people's faces, and feelings of warmth to people's hearts. We need only look around this room tonight to see that this is so. Every time I visit this school I leave a better person. People will be better for having known young men and women like these graduates.

In a few moments we will hear one of my favorite songs, "You Needed Me." Tonight's graduates, as they listen to the words of that song, will be thinking of the people they have needed, all those who have made this day possible: their parents and families who have given them life and nourished them with love; the staff, teachers and administrators of this school who have given them care and concern as well as training; the people of the community who have provided the facilities and the tools of education. We honor the graduates but, together with the graduates, we recognize that success is never the achievement of one person. Every young man and woman who graduates this spring, from whatever school or university, has needed the help of many other people along the way.

But to the honored graduates I say "We need you." The English poet John Donne wrote:

"No man is an island entire of itself; every man is part of the main.

"...if a small piece of Europe is washed into the sea all of Europe is less because of it."

We all become stronger, our nation becomes strong, as we recognize that all of us need one another.

Congratulations and God's blessings to you, graduates, and to your families. You have a right to be proud.

Q. "Why, Lord?"
A. "Love."

Being a good father to "Sunshine" during the past twenty-five years, I naturally have been very interested in her and observed her progress very closely. As each year sped by, I became more convinced that her life was not a waste but

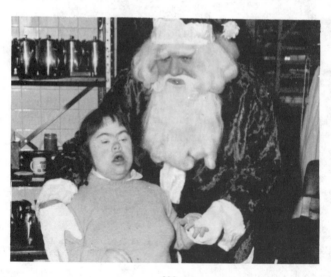

was forever shedding some power, just as a flower is steadily bestowing fragrance in the air. She may not be able to add two plus two, but to make up for this deficiency, she excels in something so many of us lack or fail to fully understand, and that is the love Jesus taught us.

As "Sunshine" grew, her love also blossomed. Personally, I cannot help but believe that the part of her brain that did not fully develop, God in His goodness and wisdom turned this "evil" into good by implanting in that void spot a so-called "sixth sense," and that was love—we might call it a sort of built-in mechanism. In "Sunshine's" love, which is so pronounced, I can see God's love so much more clearly. It is so tender, profound, forgiving, without envy or prejudice. It is a true, sincere love that is generated solely in her heart and cannot be soiled by thoughts created in her mind. Her loving heart is like a fountain of gladness, making everyone around her freshen into smiles, creating willing hearts to return her love.

I further see in "Sunshine" a special kind of love, a mini-copy of Christian love, the kind that Jesus lived and taught. It is so different from what some people understand by the word "love." It is not a love that one simply falls into or out of; Christ-like love goes beyond mere attractiveness and, when it is perfect, it even embraces those who are wicked and offensive.

Christ loves everyone, not because everyone is deserving but because it is of God to love. "God is love" (1 Jn. 4:8).

When we live in the Spirit of God, we love as Christ loves. When the Spirit lives in us, Christian love is a power we have. Love is a decision we make. Loving others is something we decide to do. It comes from the free choice of our wills, urged on by the presence of the Spirit.

If true Christian love is not something we decide to do, how can we explain Christ's command: "Love your enemies, pray for your persecutors..." (Mt. 5:44)? It is very difficult to love others when they are not nice people. How can we love someone who hates us? Or those who disagree with our way of life? How do we love those who hurt us, double-cross us, talk about us, cheat us, ignore us? We do not "fall in love" with our enemies. We are not attracted to those who make our lives difficult. These people are repulsive to us. Yet Christ says to love them. Then, of course, He Himself gave us the greatest example of all. The people of Jerusalem talked about Him, laughed at Him, discredited His preaching, misjudged Him, tried to destroy His reputation, and finally condemned Him to the most degrading death devised by man. And after all of this, with His arms outstretched on the cross, He embraces everyone and says, "This is my commandment, 'love one another as I have loved you' " (Jn. 15:12).

St. Paul in his Letter to the Corinthians writes a beautiful description of real Christian love. He says: "Set your hearts on the greater gifts. Now I will show you the way which surpasses all the others" (1 Cor. 12:31, 13:1).

"If I speak with human tongues and angelic as well, but do not have love, I am a noisy gong, a clanging cymbal. If I have the gift of prophecy and, with full knowledge, comprehend all mysteries, if I have faith great enough to move mountains, but have not love, I am nothing. If I give everything I have to feed the poor and hand over my body to be burned, but have not love, I gain nothing.

"Love is patient; love is kind. Love is not jealous, it does not put on airs, it is not snobbish. Love is never rude, it is not self-seeking, it is not prone to anger; neither does it brood over injuries. Love does not rejoice in what is wrong but rejoices with the truth. There is no limit to love's forbearance, to its trust, its hope, its power to endure" (1 Cor. 13:1-7).

Christian love is making sacrifices for others. Our Lord put it this way: "There is no greater love than this: to lay down one's life for one's friends" (Jn. 15:13). However, we may not have to give up our lives, but we can give up some of our precious time, some of our hard-earned money, some of our possessions, even our pride, for our less fortunate brothers and sisters around us, and for our neighbors in far-off poverty-stricken lands. Every good act we do is love. A smile to our neighbor is an act of love; an exhortation to our fellowman for virtuous deeds is equal to almsgiving; putting a wanderer on the right road is love; answering a call in the middle of the night to help one in need is love; visiting the elderly in nursing homes is love; changing a baby's diaper is love; forgiving is love.

To do all these things and more may not always be convenient, and the price of personal sacrifice may be extremely great. If we perform them willingly with love, even the most repulsive and arduous tasks become easy.

One exceptional thing about love is the fact that it is never lost. We may meet sometimes with ingratitude, yet love ever does a work of beauty and grace upon the heart of the giver. When we practice the love that Jesus taught us, our lives become richer and happier. When we perform a just service to our fellowman, we are rewarded with more real happiness and satisfaction than in any other venture of life. Yes, love is definitely the answer to so many of our problems.

CONCLUSION

With this we conclude the updating of "Sunshine's" story. I tried to treat everything that I thought would be of interest and importance.

All of Sunshine's brothers and sister. Back row, left to right: Robert, Albert, James. Sitting: Sunshine, Fr. Bernie, Sister Maureen. Our family—"a circle of love."

However, I am sure that there are many touching details that slipped my mind and will surely come to me after the manuscript is sent to the publisher. I must admit that writing part two, just like the first one, did not come easy. Many an hour I have spent praying to God for the proper words, not just words to fill paper, but rather, words that would flow from my heart and touch people's minds, so they, too, would profit from my experience.

In spite of my periodic fatigue in wrestling with words and sentences, I really enjoyed doing this piece of work for two reasons. First, because it is my hope that it might help my fellowman the same way my first story helped so many others. And secondly, because I also benefited from it. For by writing, some of the deeply imprinted images that were dormant in my mind were awakened.

Many of my friends have asked what motivated me to write the story of *Sunshine.* I believe that this is a good question and deserves an answer. Besides, I feel the circumstances that really generated me to write make a good human interest story.

As I previously mentioned, I never kept "Sunshine's" condition a secret from anyone. From the very beginning I spoke about her freely, and as a result of my attitude, many friends and neighbors asked me questions about Down's Syndrome which I answered to the best of my knowledge. Phil Tram, a sales representative in our Philadelphia district office, was no exception. Phil was very interested in "Sunshine" and always inquired as to how she was progressing, asking a lot of questions. I did not realize it at the time, but his exceptional, above-average interest was prompted by the fact that a very dear friend of his who worked in another office had a six-month-old child just like "Sunshine"; however, this man was bitter and ashamed that such a cruel misfortune should happen to him. He kept his daughter's condition a secret from everybody with the exception of his relatives and a few very close friends. When Phil unfolded this story to me, I felt sorry for this man and I wanted to help in some way. I asked Phil:

"Is there anything I can say or do for your friend?"

"No, Bernie," was Phil's prompt reply. "You see, he doesn't want anyone to know about his daughter; he only told me because I am considered a very close and trusted friend."

I certainly understood what Phil was telling me, and I didn't want him to break his trust, but I was searching in my mind for an alternate way to reach this troubled father. I finally struck on an idea.

"Phil, I have a book that was written by a Sister who had vast experience with these and other handicapped children. This book was a tremendous help to me, and I am sure it will help your friend. If I mail you a copy, will you forward it to your buddy?"

"I sure will! I'll be most happy to," was Phil's eager reply.

The very next day the book was on its way. I waited about two weeks before I asked Phil if he received any reaction from his friend.

"What did your friend think about the book? Did it do him any good?" I anxiously questioned.

"Yes, he received it, but I'm afraid it didn't help him. He said a couple of his relatives gave him the same book, and he didn't gain anything from it."

You can bet that I was disappointed. I thought for sure that this well-written book, composed by an expert, would have had a good effect.

I had tried and failed. But I kept thinking of the poor fellow. I couldn't get him out of my mind. I knew his agony, his discouragement, his frustration, because I had been there. There must be an answer, I kept telling myself. It was then that I got the bright idea to write my very own experience with "Sunshine." I thought if I could write my own story, as a father of a mongoloid, it might have more appeal than a professionally written script. With this thought in mind, I began my first attempt to write a story. When the manuscript was finished, I gave it the title, *I Love My Cross.* I had several copies made and gave them to my friends whom I thought would be interested. However, the very first copy was mailed to my friend Phil. Again, I waited about two weeks before I asked Phil if he had heard from his friend.

"What did your friend think of my story?" I anxiously inquired.

"Oh Bernie, I wanted to tell you, but I kept putting it off. I read your story and enjoyed it so much. I gave it to my wife to read. She, in turn, gave it to our daughter who passed it on to her cousin. Now I don't really know where it is. It will eventually show up and when it does, I will forward it to my friend. I really feel sorry about this, Bernie."

Phil was full of apologies, and I guess he had a reason to be. But frankly I wasn't thrilled about the turn of events. I was very disappointed that the troubled father did not get to read the story I wrote particularly for him. But, I guess I was a little pleased that both Phil and his family thought the story was good enough to pass around for others to read. I told Phil to keep the missing manuscript if it ever showed up, since I would send him another.

"Phil, if I send you another copy, will you promise me that you will mail it promptly to your friend?" I questioned in a serious tone.

"I sure will, Bernie. I promise it will be in his hands twenty-four hours after I receive it."

A few days later, Phil called me to let me know that the book was in the right hands this time. However, I never did learn definitely if the story helped this man to overcome his bitterness and grief. Phil never mentioned it and I never asked. I had revealed the inner workings of my soul; I felt I could do no more. The rest was up to him and God.

All the others who read the manuscript encouraged me to have it published. The Daughters of St. Paul saw value in the story and agreed to publish it. I made a few modifications and the title was changed to *Sunshine—A Slow Miracle*.

You now have the detailed account of how and why I happened to write *Sunshine—A Slow Miracle* (now Part One of this book). I certainly am not a writer, and I never had any journalistic training. But, as I have often said, God works through His people—and not always the most brilliant. If this retarded child has a message of love for all mankind, there is no better way to convey it to the multitude than through the printed word.

I also feel very strongly that when one does anything for God, even the very least thing, he never knows where it will end, nor what amount of good it will do for him. Love's secret, therefore, is to do things for God, and not be concerned because they are such very little things. Love is doing ordinary things extraordinarily well!

By writing this second part, I feel that if I have put one touch of a rosy sunset into the life of any man or woman, I shall feel that I have worked with God.

The handicapped child is not a tragedy, and neither is his birth. He is as much a loving member of a family as are the other children, AND a human person created with an immortal soul.

Finally, I want you to fully understand that just because I wrote this story with all its beautiful thoughts, I am not a saint. I am weak; I have my faults; I need your help. Therefore, in your generosity, if after you petition God for all your needs, and if you have just one little prayer left over, I sure will appreciate it if you say it for me. I thank you most sincerely.

Appendix

THE REAL CREDIT

Reading over this manuscript, I believe that I have honestly looked into my heart and have written what I saw there, earnestly hoping it will be of assistance to someone. I also reflected upon my personal blessings, blessings that I enjoy every day, yet, because they are so frequent or routine, have taken many of them for granted, forgetting to show my appreciation.

The very first and most important of these "taken-for-granted" blessings is God, and then follow His teachings and those dedicated persons to whom God sent His call to carry on His work here on earth.

Knowledge of God and His promises can change one's entire outlook on this short life here on earth. Even the most severe hardships, sufferings, and persecutions can be made tolerable and acceptable by having faith in God.

I consider myself very fortunate that I learned so much about God from my beloved parents

and guardians, who really lived their Faith and
passed it on to me. I am also most appreciative of
those Sisters of St. Joseph who put up with me
for twelve years at St. Canice School, in my
native town of Pittsburgh, Pennsylvania. They
taught me the rudiments of my Faith with
patience and loving care and had much to do
with teaching me the real values of life and how
to cope with adversity.

Although I wrote the accounts of Mary
Margaret's ("Sunshine's") life, and the amaz-
ingly good effects it had on others, the real credit
does not belong to me, but rather to the good
sisters and priests of St. Canice School, who so
long ago explained to me the love and laws of
God. I doubt very much if any of those dedicated
teachers ever had the slightest idea just how
many lives they would eventually touch through
the student who gave them so much trouble in
their religion classes. From my own personal
experience, I claim that teaching little children
about God is of the utmost importance, and those
involved in this type of education should be
highly commended. Unfortunately, it is tragic
that many teachers to do not see its unlimited
values and prefer only to communicate with
adults.

What I have learned from my religious
leaders gives me good reasons for a deep
appreciation of their work. When God spoke of
love he said, "No greater love has any man than

to give up his life for a friend." I see in our religious leaders, both men and women, this great sacrifice of love. First, for God, and secondly by generously giving of their very lives to serve God's people.

Today their work is needed more than at any other time in history. If they are to succeed in bringing the Good News of the Gospel to the world, they must have help from generous young men and women, who are being called by God for this special mission, and who willingly answer "Yes" to His call. Jesus Christ gave us the answer to the vocation shortage when He said to His Apostles, "The harvest is good but laborers are scarce. Beg the harvest master to send out laborers..." (Mt. 9:37). Therefore, all good, sincere people of all faiths should join in the spirit of ecumenical prayer to the Harvest Master to send us more laborers.

Our world is seriously sick with secularism, horrible crimes of all kinds, drug abuse, decaying morals, etc. Practices that were once labelled "unthinkable" are now considered acceptable—abortion and euthanasia. The destruction of human life, young and old, is being sanctioned on an ever-increasing scale by the medical profession, by the courts, by parents, and by silent Christians. The only sure and lasting way to cure this sickness is for the world to listen to God's Word and to put into daily practice what it hears. Our faithful religious Church leaders are the protectors and dispensers of His teachings. They are our hope, our bulwark against evil—we all need them desperately.

THE TWO TORCHES

It was the basic knowledge about the rudiments of my Faith that so often helped me to climb the high mountains and make the crooked roads straight. All through my life I enjoyed praying to God, but the church is my place of preference, because even though I cannot see Jesus behind those little tabernacle doors, my faith tells me He is truly there. And when I talk to Him, I know He is listening with concern to my sorrowful and troubled heart.

Years ago when I had driven to church after hearing that our new baby was retarded, I don't know just how long I stayed in that front pew conversing with God, but I do remember very vividly that when I left the doors of that building I felt a hundred percent better about everything.

Often I asked myself: Would my spiritual values stand the test if I personally were afflicted with a dreadful handicap or affliction?

That test came last year. Fast approaching my sixty-fifth birthday, I had been looking forward to retirement and to spending many happy years doing the things I always dreamed about but could not do while working at a steady job. All my dreams appeared to be within my grasp since I was planning to retire after forty-seven years with United States Steel. I was in perfect health—so I thought. Upon the urging of my wife, Alice, I consented to have a complete physical examination. To my great surpise this examination brought to light a tumor that was malignant.

When I first heard the word *cancer,* I thought it was impossible, that the X-ray pictures belonged to someone else. Yet, as frightful as the word cancer had been in the past, for some reason it did not upset me. Because of the values of life that I had gained from "Sunshine," my faith took over any despair that might have otherwise arisen in my mind. I had learned quite well years ago that a person needs love and faith, because they are two torches which bind their light together, and the one does not shine without the other.

The day before I was to be admitted to the hospital, Father Bernie, my son, asked me if I would like to have a private family Mass including the Sacrament of the Sick, for my intention. I was thrilled at this suggestion. I was so glad that Father Bernie thought of it since I knew that I needed all the help I could get. And the greatest and most effective help could only come from our heavenly Father. You can be sure that if I had fears harbored within me about my condition or the operation, after this ceremony I was completely fearless and relaxed for I felt everything was now in God's hands. In fact, later the family gathered around the large dining room table and we had a lot of fun joking. On Monday morning when they wheeled me from my room through the hall to the operating room I cupped my hands in such a way that when I blew into them it made a sound like an old steam locomotive. Later I was told that everyone on the floor who had heard my whistle—doctors, nurses, interns, patients and visitors alike—stopped whatever they were doing and had a big, hearty laugh. Never before had they seen a patient going to serious surgery in such a happy frame of mind.

After the operation, the doctor reported to the family that the surgery went exceptionally well, adding that as far as he could determine the surrounding areas were clear of any cancer, which was very good and welcome news.

Nobody could ever tell me that prayer and faith and love of God had nothing to do with my attitude and the successful results of my operation. I also feel that if my cancer would have been terminal it would be God's way of calling me to His heavenly home. And I would have accepted this call with love and understanding. I fully realize that some day my work here on earth will be ended and I must go to the Father.

I firmly believe that the trials of life can bring us closer to God if we permit them to do so. For this reason I think God plants fear into our souls as truly as He plants hope or courage—it is a kind of bell or gong which rings the mind into quick action for the avoidance of the approach of tragedy. It is the soul's signal for rallying and bringing more vividly into focus the reality of a loving God who wants to help us if only we return His love and seek His aid.

With each disappointment and sorrow in life I have been drawn closer to God, His saints, and His Church. With "Sunshine's" entry into my life I thought at the time that I had reached the ultimate in knowing and loving God, but this cancer brings me even closer to Him. Now I am convinced that I can never reach the peak in my love for God. In my soul there is always room for more love for Him. It is strictly up to me to nourish this love to its fullest.

"Come, all you who pass by the way, look and see whether there is any suffering like my suffering..." (Lam. 1:12)

Daughters of St. Paul

IN MASSACHUSETTS
   50 St. Paul's Ave., Jamaica Plain, Boston, MA 02130;
      617-522-8911; 617-522-0875
   172 Tremont Street, Boston, MA 02111; **617-426-5464;**
      617-426-4230
IN NEW YORK
   78 Fort Place, Staten Island, NY 10301; **212-447-5071**
   59 East 43rd Street, New York, NY 10017; **212-986-7580**
   625 East 187th Street, Bronx, NY 10458; **212-584-0440**
   525 Main Street, Buffalo, NY 14203; **716-847-6044**
IN NEW JERSEY
   Hudson Mall — Route 440 and Communipaw Ave.,
      Jersey City, NJ 07304; **201-433-7740**
IN CONNECTICUT
   202 Fairfield Ave., Bridgeport, CT 06604; **203-335-9913**
IN OHIO
   2105 Ontario St. (at Prospect Ave.), Cleveland, OH 44115; **216-621-9427**
   25 E. Eighth Street, Cincinnati, OH 45202; **513-721-4838**
IN PENNSYLVANIA
   1719 Chestnut Street, Philadelphia, PA 19103; **215-568-2638**
IN VIRGINIA
   1025 King St., Alexandria, VA 22314 **703-683-1741**
IN FLORIDA
   2700 Biscayne Blvd., Miami, FL 33137; **305-573-1618**
IN LOUISIANA
   4403 Veterans Memorial Blvd., Metairie, LA 70002; **504-887-7631;**
      504-887-0113
   1800 South Acadian Thruway, P.O. Box 2028, Baton Rouge, LA 70821
      504-343-4057; 504-343-3814
IN MISSOURI
   1001 Pine Street (at North 10th), St. Louis, MO 63101; **314-621-0346;**
      314-231-1034
IN ILLINOIS
   172 North Michigan Ave., Chicago, IL 60601; **312-346-4228**
      312-346-3240
IN TEXAS
   114 Main Plaza, San Antonio, TX 78205; **512-224-8101**
IN CALIFORNIA
   1570 Fifth Avenue, San Diego, CA 92101; **714-232-1442**
   46 Geary Street, San Francisco, CA 94108; **415-781-5180**
IN HAWAII
   1143 Bishop Street, Honolulu, HI 96813; **808-521-2731**
IN ALASKA
   750 West 5th Avenue, Anchorage AK 99501; **907-272-8183**
IN CANADA
   3022 Dufferin Street, Toronto 395, Ontario, Canada
IN ENGLAND
   128, Notting Hill Gate, London W11 3QG, England
   133 Corporation Street, Birmingham B4 6PH, England
   5A-7 Royal Exchange Square, Glasgow G1 3AH, England
   82 Bold Street, Liverpool L1 4HR, England
IN AUSTRALIA
   58 Abbotsford Rd., Homebush, N.S.W., Sydney 2140, Australia